Normal 2015

Selected Works from
The Second Annual
David Foster Wallace Conference

Copyright © 2016 Lit Fest Press

Cover Image: Copyright © 2016 Chris Ayers

All rights reserved.

ISBN: 978-1-943170-17-3

Interior Design: Jane L. Carman and Emily Brutton

Cover Image: Chris Ayers

Cover Design: Jane L. Carman

Typeface: Garamond

Published by Lit Fest Press, Carman, 688 Knox Road 900 North, Gilson, Illinois 61436

festivalwriter.org

Normal 2015

Selected Works from

The Second Annual

David Foster Wallace Conference

Carissa Kampmeier, Ashlie M. Kontos,
Brian Monday, and Emily Brutton, Eds.

Table of Contents

Introduction
  Jane L. Carman — xi

"My Wish for You": How DFW Still Teaches Me
  Brian Monday — 1

Entering the DFW Area
  Ben Leubner — 13

DFW and the Postmodern Novel of Ideas
  Rob Short — 21

Dog Stories
  Jane L. Carman — 33

Scattershot
  Amy L. Eggert — 37

"Not Another Word": Choice and Connection in *Infinite Jest*
  Carissa Kampmeier — 47

"E Unibus Pluram"—A Postscript: Applying Social Networking to DFW's Ideas Concerning Television and the Corrosive Effects of Irony
  Jeff Jarot — 55

"My Slice of Sky": Irony, Belief, and the Shadow of DFW in Letham's *Chronic City*
  David Laird — 63

A Restful Reverie (from "The Scissor Man")
   Jeffrey Calzaloia   69

Himself's Figurants
   Tom Winchester   71

Modern American Lostness (or how to be and not be alone)
   Ashlie M. Kontos   75

Dreams Are Slaughtered Here Too
   Rich Hanson   87

I'm So Totally Identifying, It's Not Even *Funny*
   Danielle S. Ely   93

The Pharmacology of *Infinite Jest* (or the deal with the missing DMZ)
   Eric Izant   99

Digital Intimacy: Art, Twitter, and DFW's *Infinite Jest*
   Corrie Baldauf   107

The Addiction Spectrum: An Analysis of the Three Branches of Addiction in DFW's *Infinite Jest*
   Emily Spalding   119

Identity Beyond Consumer Ethos in DFW's *The Pale King*
   Usama Ehsan   125

The Man Who Flew Into Space Leaves His Forthcoming Going Away Party Early Thus Putting an Abrupt End to 5.5 Years of "Academic Mobbing"
   Jodie Childers   135

Inscribing Soleas
   Alex Bertacchi Passett   137

A No That Became a (Very Long) Yes: Revisiting the
Grunge in DFW's "Grunge American Novel"
   Tony McMahon   147

Football Season's Over: Notes on a Suicide
   Ruben E. Rodriguez   157

Author Here, IYI: Preformance of Author/Text/Reader
Relationships in the Margins of DFW's Work
   Nathan Seppelt   165

Author Biographies   175

Introduction

I'd tell you all you want and more,
if the sounds I made could be what you hear.
—David Foster Wallace, *Infinite Jest*

The First Annual David Foster Wallace Conference at Illinois State University was founded as a way to celebrate the life and works of David Foster Wallace. With the generous support of the Department of English and Chair, Chris De Santis, the first conference took place in May, 2014. As we started to receive proposals, we found that the submissions were impressively varied with attendees coming from as far as Ireland, Poland, Canada, and from every corner of the US. By the second year, we added Australia, Germany, and rounded out US participation to cover all corners of the country. Wallace's influence is wide and unwavering with the list of DFW scholars transcending that of traditional academic figures including, among others, blue collar workers, lawyers, seasoned scholars with several publications, those in the medical and accounting fields, many students making their way, and former friends and colleagues of Wallace. Equally impressive was the breadth and quality of the works submitted. The conference community was inclusive, enthusiastic, inquisitive, and supportive.

It is our hope to continue to celebrate Wallace through this anthology that includes creative, critical, and hybrid works. The works included within this anthology are by no means exhaustive, rather they are meant to provide a glimpse into the varied and exciting scholarship presented at the second conference; these works hope to provide a glimpse into the stages and interest generated by Wallace, to illustrate how his work continues to influence/excite/inspire.

I would like to thank Charles B. Harris and Victoria F. Harris for sharing memories of David and for helping me make the connections necessary to get this conference off the ground. I would also like to thank the following interns and readers who made the first two conferences possible: Emily Brutton (2015), Paige Domantey (2014), Callie Dziurgot (2015), Alyssa Hanchar (2015), Mike Johnsen (2015), Carissa Kampmeier (2015), Shelly Kerker (2014), Eric Longfellow (2014), and Bryan Reid (2014).

Many thanks to the editors: Carissa Kampmeier, Ashlie Kontos, Brian Monday, and Emily Brutton for the hard work and dedication.

Without these scholars, the conferences and this anthology would not have been possible.

~Jane L. Carman, July 2016

"My Wish for You": How DFW Still Teaches Me
Brian Monday

The summer of 1996 was the original Infinite Summer[1], and one that changed me as a reader, a writer, and a future teacher. Alanis Morissette's *Jagged Little Pill* blistered the airwaves with "Ironic," that now-perpetual favorite among high school English teachers, and Baz Luhrmann's *Romeo + Juliet* played at University Cinemas, on Main Street, Normal, Illinois.

I was 24 and had just earned my bachelor's in English education at Illinois State University. Teaching positions were proving elusive, so I enrolled in David Foster Wallace's writing workshop; then due to David's encouragement, I plunged back into school to complete a master's in English studies.

The following two years of graduate school would afford me a series of heady sightings (or near sightings) of a bandana'd DFW, an array of Daves fanning out, Duchamp-like: Dave on the tennis courts at Anderson Park, accompanied by a lovely young lady, commenting on my hitting a ball against the lonely wall; Dave and perhaps the same young lady arriving late to the Luhrmann film, partway into that opening chaotic scene, and making their way down to a pair of front-row seats; Dave coming up the back steps of Stevenson Hall, from the faculty parking deck; Dave choosing (I suspect) not to answer his housedoor, where fellow grad student Kathy Peterson and I knocked to return a casebook on Cormac McCarthy's fiction he had lent us, our slipping the book through his car door's window, suspiciously cracked narrow as a drop-box slot; Dave in his office explaining that he was unable to serve as my thesis advisor, due to an upcoming sabbatical.

I feel as any student might who likewise won the academic lottery with the privilege of sitting in the classroom of one of history's literary greats but who, regrettably, didn't share his professor's eidetic memory—one of Vladimir Nabokov's students at Cornell, for example, who hadn't bothered with those style of notes that bore his alma mater's name. Then there's the rainy evening that stands out clear as an epiphany, when Dave read a lengthy

---

1   An online book club begun the summer after Wallace's death that challenged participants to read *Infinite Jest*.

passage in class from a manuscript of Don DeLillo's *Underworld*—the scene in which Father Paulus gives his charge, narrator Nick Shay as a young man, a lesson in the value of the names of things: "Sit down, Shay, and tell me how you're doing. A young man's progress. That's the title of this session" (537). I've since read this very scene aloud to *my* students, to teach them the same lesson Dave was teaching us and that DeLillo was teaching Dave and that character Father Paulus was teaching narrator Nick Shay.

But what is permanent—and what was Dave's gift to me, and the gift he gave so many of his pupils rattled into forgetfulness by the stature of their professor—is the instruction he delivered in his copious edits and in the brilliant letters he wrote by way of feedback. In such letters, Dave set before his students a perpetual model of great writing and of daunting yet inspiring lessons.

Lesson #1: Personal Connection: "This is closer to the sort of fiction I try to write…"

Dave's first letter of critique, in response to my story submission, "The Brief Journal of Marty Bean,"[2] is the longest he wrote me, and the one in which he shows the most vested interest in my writing. He begins the letter with a personal connection, then calls bullshit on 80% of the story, and finally softens this blow with sincere concern for my growth as a writer. He undergirds the letter with brilliant analysis and a knowledge of the story that surpassed my own.

In my story a fledgling writer, Marty, keeps track of new words he's learned (in reading the work of Faulkner) and begins a story within the story that acts allegorically for his own fraught relationship with his father. Dave's opening gambit of response is forceful and nuanced: "This is closer," he writes, "to the sort of fiction I try to write than some of the other stories are. Surprisingly, this makes me read it tougher and w/ less charity than a sweet realist tale of collegiate romance…." That Dave would draw this comparison between my fiction and his own felt like he'd bent down from his great height and cupped his hands to give me a much-needed boost. He was acknowledging a kinship along aesthetic lines. What's more, the qualifying clause "I try to write" reveals Dave's humility, as it implies a struggle and occasional failure on his part to succeed in writing this "sort of fiction," the sort that plays games with its reader. But perhaps Dave opened his letter this way less to lift me up than to prepare me for a knockdown. After all, I was drunk on metafiction, that icy draft of self-consciousness, and was attempting to play a literary game whose rules I hardly knew. I was constructing my private little house of cards that

---

2 Dave was suspicious of the word "brief." "Why *brief?*" he asked. I now suspect that he was busy writing *Brief Interviews with Hideous Men*.

refused to "become a castle of beautiful steel and glass" (Nabokov 6). I'd forgotten I'd invited the reader over, was now fumbling the cards—they were falling out my sleeve—and Dave, my guest, was there to call out the sham.

Lesson #2: Insult, Compliment, Deep Analysis: "It's bullshit, but bullshit of a rather sophisticated sort..."

And then comes the knockdown, a complex blend of compliment and insult: "My overall take on this is that it's bullshit, but bullshit of a rather sophisticated sort, with about 25% great writing." My translation, for my high school students, might read: "My overall take on your story is that it doesn't ring true...." But what a limp alternative to Dave's coldcock version: "it's bullshit," so punchy and true. Then there's the immediate blow-softening compliment: "but bullshit of a rather sophisticated sort," and the even more flattering, "with about 25% great writing."

But why bullshit? Dave will go on to critique the overwritten quality of the story—of how its narrative layers, the stories within the story, don't add up to any clear experience for the reader, how I've cleverly crafted my story around Biblical themes of sight and blindness to preempt my reader's potential criticisms. As Dave puts it:

> When we ask...why there's so little on Marty's Mom and Dad...the story can reply that it's all a very esoteric parable, that we "see" but do not "perceive." Clever but dangerous—because what you've done is use your cleverness to defend the story against criticism instead of doing the harder, less clever work of actually making some of the above confusions add up to something.

Dave ends his critique of my second story submission—"Textbook Metaphors"—with a confession that he is tempted by the same siren's song: "I myself have trouble with showing off, because I think I too can write really eyepoppingly good prose when I want." Dave's criticism of my attempted style is deeply ironic, as his style is likewise highly metafictional, an irony Dave overtly acknowledges, but seeing this flaw in his students' work likely accelerated his awareness and correction of it in his own. Dave speaks to this mentor-mentee dynamic in a 1996 interview with Leonard Lopate:

> I've learned more teaching in the last three years than I ever learned as a student. And a lot of it is that when you see students work where the point...is basically that they're clever, and to try and articulate to the student how empty and frustrating it is for a reader.... All the kind of stuff, right, when I'm doing my little onanistic, clever stuff in grad school...I would go, "Well, they don't understand. I'm a genius...." Now that I'm the teacher, I'm starting to learn...that they had some smart stuff to tell me.

In my case, Dave was giving me more credit (or discredit) for cleverness than I deserved. What he saw as wily intent was closer, at best, to a blind but earnest swipe at something like the kind of fiction I most admired, or was, at worst, the result of an impulsive, if modestly inspired, sloppy copy from a writer who hadn't yet learned to ask the deeper questions: What *are* my characters' motives? Why *have* I chosen this level of diction? How *will* my reader find meaning in the end? What Dave helped me to *perceive* was that fiction is an act of communication, if of an artistic kind, and a key method he used in conveying this message was his honest, distinctive blend of pseudo-insult and compliment. He leads with a two-toned insult—half play, half urgency—to command his pupil's attention, and once had, he then props his reeling pupil back up and makes him believe there's no ceiling on his potential. One hears the scroop of chair legs across the floor, as the teacher firmly pulls his student to his side.

Lesson #3: Meticulous Editing: "The next time you use only Spell Checker to proofread…I'll grade you down…. I shit you not."

While confusing one's homonyms might seem a proofreading peccadillo to most, for Dave such an offense was great. He ends his critique of my first submission with the closing "Go and sin no more," delivered in equal parts playful overstatement and sincere absolution, in reference to my proofreading sins and other graver transgressions. Dave's fanaticism regarding grammar and usage is well-covered terrain (Boswell 2-3, Max 3-7). Dave's mother, Sally Foster, in her introduction to the "Teaching Materials" portion of *The David Foster Wallace Reader*, describes their shared process of reading a student's essay three times—Dave using a different color ink with each pass. She also produces samples of Dave's syllabi, one of which contains a footnote elaborating, "Written work with excessive typos, misspellings, or basic errors in usage/grammar will not be accepted…. If you believe this is just the usual start-of-term saber-rattling, be advised that some of the students in this course have had me as an instructor before—ask them whether I'm serious" (611). In the Lopate interview, Dave glosses his reputation as militant enforcer of proper grammar: "the only way that I'm well known at Illinois State is that I am the 'grammar Nazi.' And so any student whose deployment of a semi-colon is not absolutely Mozart-esque knows that they're going to get a C in my class."

Dave's marginal comments on a single submission could range from the harsh to the gentle. In an exchange in the Facebook group "Former Students of David Foster Wallace," Lynn Bulgrin recalls: "I vividly remember him drawing a line on one of my stories and writing something to the effect of 'Shitty from this point on.'" On another submission of hers, however, he provided the addendum, "Couldn't resist marking it up!," signed by the gentle-sounding "Style Fairy." In this same Facebook thread, Kate Colbert writes: "He used playful comments and smiley faces to 'soften'…his other harsh commentary," a remembrance that sparked a rash of DFW smiley-face shares. His edits as often deal with deeper problems, such as problematic point-of-view shifts and inconsistent diction levels. I finally understood, through Dave's corrections, the elasticity of point of view, how a writer can put the reader just over a character's shoulder or take her far above, as well as the continuum of diction levels available to a writer, from "colloquial" to "fancy." On occasion his edits include a personal touch: for example, I'd long forgotten that I'd sent him to the dictionary, a little badge of honor, for a definition of "coruscations," a word I'd just learned from Faulkner, above which he writes, as surprised as I, "I looked it up!"

On my first story submission Dave put pen to paper 170 times, for an average of just over 10 marks per page, and 84 edits on my second story, for an average of 14 marks per page. The exceptional fact is that Dave then also wrote typed letters that each filled a page to a page and a half. What's more, he then copy edited his letters, modeling the proofreading process. The clear message was that even the guru makes mistakes and no project is too small to merit meticulous proofreading: each text we write, whether a personal letter or an email, communicates our education, our love of the language, and our respect for the reader.

Lesson #4: Writing as an Act of Communication: the Teacher *Schools* His Pupil—"Yes, Grasshopper, I too can sling the lingo…."

There are unmistakable flashes in Dave's letters of his intent to show me *who was schooling whom*, as when he writes: "The Barthian metafictional recursions and semiotic layerings and hermeneutic circles (yes, Grasshopper, I too can sling the lingo) here seem (to me) to be…hiding the fact that much of the first 13 pages is…more like the ground-clearing for a novel than a tight cool story." I had read Barth's *Lost in the Funhouse*, but I couldn't "sling the lingo" or create "recursions and semiotic layerings and hermeneutic circles" the way Dave gives me credit for. His language targets and throws back at me the very aspect of my writing that was out of control and that Dave knew the dangers of. His overt and playful reference to the David Carradine character, Caine, or "Grasshopper," in the TV series *Kung Fu*, admits the potentially adversarial mentor-mentee apprenticeship whose sparring threatens to get out of hand, requiring the master to drub the grasshopper.

I never responded to Dave's critiques—either in writing or in person—and we certainly never chewed the hermeneutic fat or shot the semiotic shit. This fact, to me, is a testament to the power and longevity of a letter. When Bryan

A. Garner begins his interview[3] with the question, "What's the best way to learn to write well?," Dave's answer focuses on the writer's relationship with his reader:

> writing well means to communicate clearly and interestingly and in a way that feels alive to the reader. Where there's some kind of relationship between the writer and the reader—even though it's mediated by a kind of text—there's an electricity about it.... (26)

Dave's critiques retain all the "electricity" of a personal, face-to-face conference. Later in the interview Dave reflects on the value of such letters—"It was in college...when I had professors who...would, in fact, write mini-letters of response...that I realized that my papers were intended to be communications" (33)—and then reflects, again, on the relationship between author and reader:

> really learning how to write effectively is...more of a matter of spirit than it is of intellect.... And the spirit means I never forget there's someone on the end of the line, that I owe that person certain allegiances, that I'm sending that person all kinds of messages. (35)

And indeed, Dave's critiques sent "all kinds of messages" to me, one of which was that I had forgotten to honor the "allegiances" I owed my reader, and his yanking on "the other end of line," his drubbing the grasshopper, was his spirited way of communicating to me what he knew I needed most to hear.

Lesson #5: A Broader Context: "For the most part Marty reminds me of O'Connor's...Julian *sans* any kind of epiphanic realization that he's full of shit."

In response to my two story submissions, Dave references Barth ("Ambrose His Mark"), Faulkner ("Quentin in *Absalom*"), O'Connor ("Everything that Rises Must Converge"), *Moby-Dick*, Tolkien[4], and *Dead Poets Society*. That these works and my drafts were worlds apart in caliber was understood. But the references located key stories and novels on Dave's bookshelf that were touchstones for him. They served to place his students' drafts into some relation to texts he knew intimately well and that aided his analysis and assessment of them. They also provided his students similar frames of reference—for understanding their submissions in new ways, relative to masterworks—and if they hadn't yet read a given author or title, they were implicitly invited to do so. In creating these contexts, Dave let his students know that their attempts at fiction mattered, and that they fit, however askew, into a tradition of conventions and techniques and perceptions of human experience.

---

3 Published in *Quack This Way*.
4 My second story made use of allusions to Ahab and Frodo.

Lesson #6: Aesthetic Underpinnings and Far-Reaching Wisdom: "It takes courage and self-awareness and discipline to *use* the good writing instead of being used *by* it."

The crux of Dave's criticism comes down to the fundamentals: the writer's relationship to the reader, her control over impulses to show off, her ability to create a story that "adds up" to something greater than the sum of its parts, and her understanding of the demands that the avant-garde places on her reader. For all of the technical intricacies of Dave's own fiction, he is surprisingly traditionalist in his criticism of my submissions. He recounts, in the Lipsky interview, his own experience facing traditionalist backlash against his avant-garde submissions (47). But Dave learned to "write with his spine," to strike a balance between the "algebra" and the "fire," as Nabokov and Barth respectively put it[5]. He learned to undergird the "clever semiotic layerings" with some true communication about human experience—about loneliness and sadness—and in such a way as to evoke a powerful response in his reader. Dave learned to strip away all the layers to reveal a true, added-up-to-something something underneath. Dave's aesthetics are summed up well in the following passage from his critique of my first story submission:

> Why on earth you chose to give us so little on Dad when it's...his fundamentalism that seems to motivate...Marty's hyperliterary stuntpilotry...is beyond me. I do know that developing a plausible, emotionally resonant relation between the two—a relation that would make Marty's character more 3D by locating his rather jejune literary pretensions in a human, universal antipathy/adulation thing with a parent—would be far harder than the clever semiotic layerings and intertextual hooha you've put in to avoid doing the work.... (I am far from free of precisely the same desires to show off and cheat and replace inglorious character development with glorious formal tricks.)

No doubt Dave privileged style, and while he reviewed my second story, "Textbook Metaphors," much more favorably—"Again, a creative, fantasy-prone young man is opposed by establishment/parental forces on issues of literary relevance. But this is better, tighter."—he dinged it, too, for its overwritten quality. The story puts the reader very tightly in the character's perspective—his name is Jason—and traces his near-trance-like daydreams as he sits through class. The story tries, unsuccessfully, to warrant its level of description, but as Dave rightly argues, the daydreams are implausibly intense and lack any integral relation to character. "Jason's daydreams," he writes, "are either psychotic hallucinations or else nearly mystical states.... What's up with them? How do they relate to Jason's character?" He then reaches the following conclusions:

---

5 Nabokov actually uses the phrase "with one's spine" in regard to *reading*.

> You don't tell us—you just try to blow our socks off with the lapidary gorgeousness of the daydreams themselves. But this makes the daydream conceit (as in "wild conceit" from *M-D*) seem like basically a set-up.... The only way really good writing that calls attention to itself as good writing escapes smelling of show-offery is if it has a clear deep integral relation to character and story. Here it doesn't— you haven't done the work required to make it integral. It stands by itself, for the most part, 80% gorgeous, 20% clunky or purple...but always looking...pleased with itself.

My story's language "belonged," as James Wood puts it in *How Fiction Works*, much more to me than to my character, which resulted in a style "looking annoyingly authorial" (26-29). Wood acknowledges that a blend of an author's own style and his characters' natural language is desired: "Shakespeare's characters sound like themselves and always like Shakespeare, too." He cites Wallace as a "contemporary writer [who] wants to push this tension to the limit": "He writes from within his characters' voices and simultaneously over them, obliterating them in order to explore larger...questions of language" (30-31). Wood thinks Wallace's style "fairly ugly, and a bit painful for more than a page or two," citing a passage from "The Suffering Channel," but Wood's assessment here is myopic, leaving out the vital qualification that Wallace's style is elsewhere so often "lapidary" and "eyepoppingly good." Wood does recognize, however, that Wallace's fiction "prosecutes a courageous argument about the decomposition of language in America" and that Wallace is "not afraid to decompose—discompose—his own style in the interests of making us live through this linguistic America with him" (33). How Dave's fiction succeeds in its highly-stylized nature is, again, that it *communicates* to the reader some profound meaning; it *adds up* to something far beyond its own veneer of style. Perhaps a writer's odds of accomplishing such a communication are increased over the course of a career, of a body of work; the writer has *earned* the right to a style that calls attention to itself, has built a solid case for that style, and the reader is assured, going in, of a reward.

While my second story demonstrated my concerted effort to improve, I still hadn't learned the lesson Dave was trying to impart, and so he ends his second letter, as he did his first, on a cautionary note:

> It takes courage and self-awareness and discipline to *use* the good writing instead of being used *by* it [emphasis Dave's].... I occasionally have this courage; when I don't, my writing ends up looking talented but immature, exhibitionistic. Thousands of people can write gorgeous prose; far fewer can write a really good story. From this and the other piece, I'd say you're in the former camp but not yet in the latter. It'd be interesting to see your struggles with yourself over the

next decade. My wish for you is that they be quicker and less painful than my own have been.

I wish I could say I've mastered Dave's lessons, and that he truly would have found my subsequent struggles "interesting." I don't know that I've found the kind of courage Dave means. But what James Wood calls "ugly" about Dave's story might very well be Dave's courageously and finally stripping it all down. After all, his closing confessional aside to me is interestingly written in the present tense—"I occasionally have this courage…"—suggestive of his continued struggle to be "self-disciplined" in his writing. Perhaps in "The Suffering Channel" and the other *Oblivion* stories Dave had reached a final show of courage effecting a style that was perhaps as painful to write as it was (for James Wood, anyway) to read.

Lesson #7: The True Teacher: "My wish for You…"

Dave's final lesson to me extends beyond the question of fiction writing, and that is *to love teaching*. To devote generous amounts of time to students and their work. To know their talents, and to nurture those talents. Dave lived this lesson. What student wouldn't respond to a teacher who says or writes to him, "My wish for you…"?[6] While Dave might not have reached every student—no teacher does—he approached teaching with the same intelligence, dedication, and rigor as he did his writing, and he deeply impacted his students and colleagues, as born witness to in the beautiful tributes delivered at a memorial service held at Illinois State University, November 1, 2008.[7] From Brian W. Budzynski's memory of giving Dave a ride home after class, stopping at a gas station for Dave to buy himself dinner (peanut butter and white bread) (26), to Lynn Bulgrin's ending her beautiful memorial with a personal address: "There are so many things I'd like to say and share about you, but the essence of what I'm trying to express is that your students loved you and will continue to" (28); from Chris Paddock's memory of the same McCarthy-DeLillo-Gaddis-and-Gass lit. class in which Dave read from *Underworld*: "He accomplished something else through this class. He helped demystify himself as an icon in our eyes, something that, looking back, seemed to be terribly important to him…" (68), to Marty Riker's remarkable recollection of the evening he helped Dave find a deer he had hit with his car, on a return trip from a visit at John O'Brien's (74). Dave's peers offer similar testaments. Mary Caponegro writes, "Unlike so many writers who regard teaching as a necessary evil…

---

6   In recently reading Rilke's *Letters to a Young Poet* for the first time, I was struck by Rilke's repeated expression of his wishes for Franz Xaver Kappus: "your life, dear Mr. Kappus, I think of it with so many wishes for you…and send you wishes…. It is always my wish…" (82, 88).

7   Later collected in a volume titled *Remembering David Foster Wallace*.

Dave was earnestly and humbly invested…" (89). Of teaching with him, Becky Bradway writes, "I can't imagine teaching that well with anybody else. And it wasn't because I was deferential. In fact, I'd say quite the opposite" (21).[8]

But teaching must have also eaten into Dave's creative energies and resources. In reference to writing *Infinite Jest*, he told Lipsky, "I literally could not teach and do it at the same time" (2). To Charlie Rose, he explained the potentially dead-end challenges teaching poses:

> The teacher learns a lot more than the students. You do for about two or three years and then the curve falls off sharply. And most of the older teachers that I know, except for a very few geniuses, are extremely bored with teaching, and they're going through the motions…. And the more time spent on teaching, which is extraordinarily hard to do well, the less time spent…on your own work.

That Dave went on to teach another ten years, beyond that three-year threshold he describes, says a great deal about the rewards he found in teaching.

David Lipsky depicts what was perhaps one of Dave's final interactions with a set of students, the spring before his suicide: "In early May, he sat down at a cafe with some graduating seniors from his fiction class. He answered their jittery, writer's-future questions. At the end, his voice went throaty, he choked up. Students assumed he was joking—some smiled, a memory that would cut later. David sniffled. 'Go ahead and laugh—here I am crying—but I really am going to miss all of you'" (xviii). Lipsky's account is evidence that Dave's devotion as a teacher, and his impact, extended to his position at Pomona College and never waned.

"Good teachers," Dave's mother writes, "are those who so love their subjects that they try with all their might and main to help students love them, too, forever" (601). As one of Dave's former students, I can attest that this is exactly what he did.

A Summary of DFW Lessons…

---

8 I specifically remember Becky's distaste for my habit of recycling certain gags in a story, and Dave's defense of this device, saying that he, too, would ride a working gag as long as he could; conversely I remember Becky's defense of my second story submission's ending, "Textbook Metaphors," that Dave felt was too sentimental, ending as it did with a character writing poems on the soles of his shoes, but that Becky felt hit the correct inspirational note, saying that she'd put on Paul Simon's "Diamonds on the Soles of Her Shoes" after finishing my story, a comment I relished hearing.

It's been nearly 20 years since Dave was my teacher. In the years since, I've intermittently reflected on his impact and read and reread his work, but it seems fitting that this spring I finally committed, after years of hesitation, to teaching Wallace's *The Broom of the System* to my AP English seniors. My reservations about teaching *Broom* to high schoolers were many, but my students immediately responded to Dave's voice, to his blend of stratospheric vocabulary with the casual or even vulgar. From the first sentence on, they were immersed. They found the novel relatable and hip. They enjoyed its unfinished final sentence—"I'm a man of my   "—and, nearly to a student, cited it as their favorite book of the year. We studied it as we would any other novel, for all the same elements of character and theme, but also as we *would no other*.

In teaching *Broom*, and in preparing this paper for the second annual David Foster Wallace Conference, I'm left freshly aware of the role Dave played in my education. His lessons continue to resonate: writing instruction is best delivered with a personal but sometimes brutally honest touch, supported by deep understanding of the merits and demerits of a student's writing and her inclinations; a teacher should demonstrate competency in every word spoken in class or jotted in the margins of a draft; he should situate a student's work within a rich network of contexts, part of which is his (the teacher's) own wisdom and aesthetic; he should care about his students and invest in them and teach them that grammar matters and that, above all, writing is about establishing and maintaining a relationship with the reader and conveying something coherent and meaningful to that reader.

What luck and what honor—first to have been one of Dave's students and now to teach one of his novels, and to try, at least in the classroom, to follow in his giant, recursive, playful, plodding, earnest, big-brother, barely-earth-treading bootsteps. David Foster Wallace was truly a man, and a teacher, of his

Works Cited

Boswell, Marshall. *Understanding David Foster Wallace*. 2003. Columbia, SC: U. of South Carolina Press, 2009. Print.

Bulgrin, Lynn. "I vividly remember." 27 Jan., 5:57 PM. Facebook post.

Colbert, Kate. "He used playful comments." 27 Jan., 12:36 PM. Facebook post.

DeLillo, Don. *Underworld*. New York: Scribner, 1997.

Lipsky, David. *Although Of Course You End Up Becoming Yourself: A Road Trip with David Foster Wallace*. New York: Broadway Books, 2010.

Foster, Sally. "Teaching Materials." Introduction. *The David Foster Wallace Reader*. New York: Little, Brown and Company, 2014. Print.

Garner, Bryan and David Foster Wallace. *Quack This Way*. Dallas: Penrose, 2013. Print.

Max, D. T. *Every Love Story Is a Ghost Story*. New York: Viking, 2012.

Nabokov, Vladimir. "Good Readers, Good Writers." *Lectures on Literature*. Ed. Fredson Bowers. New York: Harcourt, 1980. Print.

Rilke, Maria Rainer. *Letters to a Young Poet*. Trans. Joan M. Burnham. Novato: New World Library, 2000. Print.

Wallace, David Foster. *The Broom of the System*. London: Penguin, 2004. Print.

---. Letters to author. 2006. TS.

---. Interview with Leonard Lopate. WNYC *Leonard Lopate Show*. 1996.

---. Interview with Charlie Rose. *Charlie Rose*. 27 Mar. 1997. Web. 20 April 2015.

Wood, James. *How Fiction Works*. New York: Picador. 2008. Print.

Entering the DFW Area
Ben Leubner

Not to be "terminally unique"
Will be the consolation you take home.
—James Merrill, "Family Week at Oracle Ranch"

It wasn't until recently that I began to read David Foster Wallace.

I've always been a bit slow on catching up with what's happening in the present. As a teenager growing up in the northwest in the early 1990's, I even scoffed, initially, at the prospect of Nirvana. Were it not for a friend in high school, I wouldn't have experienced Nirvana in concert in January of 1994, when I was fifteen, just three months before Kurt Cobain's own suicide.[1]

When working Saturdays at a new and used books and vinyl store in Bozeman, Montana, I often occupy myself, especially during the slow winter months, by pulling books off the shelves and reading them for a while behind the counter: mountaineering chronicles, contemporary political commentary,

---

1   Wallace was five years older than Cobain, but Cobain was gone two years before *Infinite Jest* appeared, during the composition of which Wallace was listening to a good deal of Nirvana. The two figures have surely been brought up in the same sentence plenty of times, usually a sentence, I imagine, about how Wallace's suicide seemed reminiscent of Cobain's, both being cases of the sudden disappearance of the "voice of a generation." But there's another similarity besides and more important than the abrupt and sad endings, namely, the shared experience of sudden fame and the helplessly falling into a depression as a result of it, a depression that generated, in both cases, an intense skepticism regarding mass media and the American entertainment industry as well as the realization through painful experience that substance abuse contributed to more than it alleviated depression. This actually happened to Wallace *before* it happened to Cobain, after the success of his first novel, when he was roughly the same age that Cobain was when it happened to him, though Wallace's success at this stage of his career was nothing, of course, compared to the rock and roll superstardom into which Cobain found himself precipitously and terrifyingly launched. Still, there's no doubting that Wallace was intimately familiar with the idea, as Nietzsche formulated it, of celebrity as a kind of punishment that masquerades as public festivity.

potboiler thrillers with recurring heroes, western American landscape narratives—whatever attracts me in a given moment. It was thus that I finally began to read Wallace, as a sense of an obligation to read him broke through the surface of my consciousness and was no longer something I felt compelled to willfully resist.

As my shifts went by, I slowly made my way through the nonfiction. I began to look forward to Saturdays at the store solely so that I could continue reading Wallace (at first, I never took any of his books home). I'd come in on a snowy morning, shake off my boots, turn on the lights, and make sure that everything was in order: check all of the display shelves, straighten the LPs, and put on some jazz from the 1920s. Then, once we were open, I'd make my way to the back right corner of the store, where the Ws, Ys, and Zs hide out in the shadows. From a bottom shelf a single tier beneath Vonnegut (the tyranny of alphabetization often plays such jokes), I would tip out one of the books of essays and carry it back to the front of the store. It can sometimes be as long as an hour or two on those winter Saturdays before the first customer comes in, so my mornings would often start with nothing but coffee, jazz, and David Foster Wallace.

In all these first few months, though, I never once touched *Infinite Jest*, though I knew, of course, of its existence.

Then one night in early 2014, quite possibly twenty years to the day after I saw Nirvana in the Spokane Arena, I dreamt that I was at a party in a darkly lit room in which indistinct people were milling about on the pressing peripheries of my vision. I felt a particularly dreamlike discomfort at finding myself in their midst, able to make out only a wall here and a corner there for the shadows of their faces. Emerging somehow out of this nebulous interior, Wallace appeared in clear relief, put his arm around my shoulder, and said, "We should talk sometime."

Now, I was neither naively accepting of this dream *nor* totally dismissive of it. That is to say, I did not enthusiastically subscribe to the possibility that what had been said had in fact been conveyed in some sense by some ethereal manifestation of Wallace himself, but I didn't wholly dismiss this as a possibility, either. I've heard it said that the dead are always themselves in dreams, but it's not like I felt that David Foster Wallace wanted to be my friend or that his ghost was selecting me as some kind of chosen one. As James Merrill to my ears more plausibly suggests, these kinds of voices, while we should never entirely dismiss the ways in which they indeed seem to originate outside ourselves, are surely also ("also," not "really") voices that come from within, aspects of our own selves that cloak themselves in whatever fashion is necessary—the voices of the dead, perhaps—in order for our waking selves to actually be given a chance to heed them.

The utterance, "We need to talk," then, meant, in essence, that I knew enough from what I'd already read that Wallace had some fairly profound thoughts on both the necessity of perpetually decentering and thereby diminishing one's own ego *and* how to go about doing this—and that this was something I needed to do. For constantly considering yourself at the center of things is a perilous business; it induces a dual sense of both importance and isolation: the ego reinforces itself by vacuuming everything towards and into it, all the while complaining of the desolate waste by which it is then surrounded. This was *anti*-nirvana, as far as I could tell, something the avoidance of which I considered both paramount and extremely difficult, perhaps even impossible in my own life. In a sense, then, I was trying to assign Wallace to myself as a kind of coach who might be able to help me work through these straits and thus finally, narrowly escape a recurring self-centered bitterness I was only too eager to leave behind but which I constantly felt was simply and inevitably in my blood. The infamous 27 had come and gone with little to no anxiety for me, but 46 was and still is an entirely different, much larger and darker, bear in the woods.

Thus, in the small burst of a mildly stunned early morning moment, I realized what this dream meant: it meant that I finally needed to read *Infinite Jest*. But I was currently in the midst of a three-course semester, so as much as I wanted to begin reading the novel immediately, I thought, at first, that I'd better hold off until the summer; I'd take the book with me on a trip to France and begin reading it while sitting outside at cafes and in parks, among ashtrays and toy boats. What I didn't realize, however, was that by this time such decisions were out of my hands; the novel was zeroing in on me with all the sureness of a leviathan. Soon it would swallow me whole; in my own calendar of subsidized time, 2014 would become the YDFW, or, as it turned out, the Year of *Infinite Jest*.

In mid-February I received a call from a school in Boston that wanted to interview me for a job, and I agreed to fly out to a city I'd spent five years living in while working on my PhD and had never really liked much. So I began preparing for the interview, researching the school and its faculty, and talking myself into the viability of the position. The school looked dynamic, the faculty appealing. A week before I left, though, and not quite knowing why, as I already had plenty going on in my life, I pulled *Infinite Jest* off the shelf just to read a few pages out of curiosity in a moment of downtime, just before bed one night. There would have been a fire going inside and snow falling outside, and I would have fallen into one of those interstices where one is incapable of doing any of the things one feels obligated to do. I would have wanted to simply sit on the couch, open a book, and read for an hour, without any thought whatsoever as to what use I would then make of what I was reading in the classroom tomorrow.

As soon as I picked up the book I became suddenly very curious about it: what was its first sentence? how did its first "chapter" unfold? just how stylistically compact would it turn out to be? and so on. Also, what was the meaning, on some of the pages, of these small, centered, somewhat three-dimensional circles that resembled a number of things, most pertinently, perhaps, both tennis balls and pills, each one a kind of closed circuit or loop, a white circle cupped by a dark crescent, a bouncing ball that seems to be in the process of falling off of the novel-proper's last page before the "Notes and Errata"?

While it opens in Arizona, most of the novel takes place in a dystopian Boston, which is to say, Boston. The first 27 pages of the book were enough for me to realize and confirm this, just enough, also, to get, if not hooked, at least still more curious than I'd been when I first picked it up, and so interested enough to decide to take the book to Boston with me. I didn't know how much of it I would read while I was there. I certainly didn't know that the entire purpose of the trip would shift radically as a result of bringing a certain book with me, that it would turn into a literary trip in, what, all three senses of the word: trip, trip, and trip? Yes: a literal voyage on which I stumbled into a life-altering experience. In the end, I would read something else in France and Switzerland.

Often the seemingly secondary or tertiary ends up being, or at least wanting to be, the primary, while what we're often conditioned to consider the primary is of no importance at all. Sometimes the universe makes you wonder in these ways. You wonder if, while you're busy trying to accommodate various things within it, it's not busy trying in some manner to arrange things in specific ways for you, ways that cut against the very grain you yourself are so adamantly trying to establish. Reading the next 213 pages of the novel (up to page 240, total) before returning to Bozeman would turn out, in retrospect, to have been the entire purpose of the trip. The job interview (the school depressing, the faculty interviewing me covered dourly in the dust of several decades) was an agonizing exercise in spewing by rote; there was no conversation whatsoever. Before it was even halfway over, when I should have simply left, I had already convinced myself that it was, in fact, nothing more than the excuse that had been needed to get me to Boston for four days. The idea would have been something like this: I needed to read as much of *Infinite Jest* as possible while riding the Green Line's "B" trolley back and forth from the city center to Chestnut Hill, along which route lie the locales of the novel's twin fictive hearts, Enfield Tennis Academy and the Ennet Recovery House. Then, an excuse was needed to convert the idea into a reality, as it never would have occurred to me to think, "Hey, I think I'll drop everything for a weekend, go to Boston, and read a book there." Hence, the job interview. The question of who's responsible for all of this choreography often keeps me up at night.

Ostensibly, then, the trip had been about my trying to secure a new job; that's what I told people: "I'm going to Boston for a job interview this weekend." But even as it was still ongoing, I became sure that the trip had really, from the beginning, had no other point than to provide me with the ideal space in which to begin reading a particular novel that I'd been putting off reading for well over a decade. Explaining *this* to others without having them look back at me quizzically was somewhat more difficult, so I kept it for the most part to myself. The paradox is that "I'm going to Boston for a job interview" hints at the idea of a simple reality the existence of which we daily delude ourselves into affirming, while "I went to Boston to read a book" was a fiction I ended up creating out of the experience, a pattern I wove into the fabric of my experience by way of retrospective contemplation, but a fiction and a pattern that demanded precedence over mere reality precisely by virtue of their seeming, well, much more real than it. It is somewhat solipsistic and self-absorbed, yes, the retroactive fabrication that all of Boston was at my disposal for four days, the whole city preternaturally orchestrated in order to create an ideal reading environment that would accommodate me alone. But this orchestration consisted of nothing more than the city simply going on as it always does; I was as much at its disposal as it was at mine. It's not quite solipsism, that is, if you consider yourself a part *of* the fiction of the world, and not apart *from* it.

But to take things even a little further: it wasn't simply that I was flying to Boston in order to read, largely unbeknownst to myself at the time I set out, 200+ pages of *Infinite Jest* over the course of a long weekend, so that I could then finish the book by Easter. Even this particular spin on things is too tame, doesn't have enough slice, as it were. What *really* happened was that when I boarded the plane that would take me from Minneapolis to Boston, I was also boarding a plane that would take me from reality to fiction, and not to Logan but to the DFW area, as I would spend the next four days not so much merely in the city in which Wallace sets most of *Infinite Jest*, but in the realm of *Infinite Jest* itself, in *its* Boston, so that whenever a character heard, on this page or that, the rumble of the B as it lurches its way towards Chestnut Hill, I might have been on that very train reading just that passage at just that time. That is, I somehow survived entrance into the atmosphere of a fictive realm that Wallace had carefully laid over or thrust under habitual reality, and I was now *in* the novel as opposed to just into it. From the trolleys I rode I might have gazed out the windows towards the hill where Enfield and Ennet are located; in fact, I often craned my neck and turned my head around precisely for the purpose of doing so, and there they were, plainly revealed to me despite being hidden by buildings and trees, and despite not actually being there according to the dictates of the pesky and paltry real.

All around me were signs of waste being marshaled for removal to the Great Concavity; nearby was the football stadium where the Allston Wolf Spiders played; there was the bar in which the senior students of the tennis academy were sometimes allowed to drink. As for the Entertainment itself, it was all around me, in the form of people, including myself, seemingly unable to pull themselves away from phones and tablets, people who, were they to carry their various addictions to, fetishes for, and obsessions with their technology to their furthest reaches, never would. You can read *Infinite Jest* on your tablet, but you can also *watch* it there, or rather, watch myriad variations upon it, all of them imperfect reflections of the superform of the film itself. But Reading *Infinite Jest* is quite different from watching it, though there is a considerable overlap between the two, and it is as beguiling an atmospheric borderland as the one that exists between reality and fiction.

The 1996 novel's not too distant future is now obviously our past, but it is also still our present just as it was in 1996, and yet remains our future. The various ways in which its fiction interfaces with our lives renders the very distinction between reality and fiction, where the two are habitually considered mutually exclusive, an utter fallacy. Was I in good old, clear-cut reality, reading a book about a film on a green line trolley? Or was I in the reality of the book, itself a fiction, with the film, or lesser versions of it, anyway, all around me, threatening to engulf? Or was I perhaps even in the film, reading within it the book that gave rise to it, hopelessly lost, now, to that good old reality that was itself no doubt the greatest illusion, the most infinite jest, of them all? I was beset by vortices of virtuality, set just as free on their various surfaces as I was limited by their spiraling pull. There are any number of virtual worlds capable of transfixing us; some of them both require and demand our initiative while others seek only to dissolve it, only it's often strangely difficult to tell the difference between the alleviation of loneliness through activity and its engendering through passive reception.

Infinite Jest itself is infinite, containing within its confines deep wells and endless corridors of thought that are both empty and dazzling, full of literary dark matter by virtue of which the words that actually constitute the novel proper could be said to comprise only a thousandth of its larger breadth, its greater quantum sprawl that both generates and receives us as we read. As if to corroborate this sense of expanse, the weight of the book itself, especially a hardcover edition, is considerable; it will sit heavy in any bookbag or satchel, like an original tablet of the sort people carried down from mountaintops, causing a strain not only on the shoulder but also, once one has started reading it, on the brain. Add to its weight, in this particular instance, a journal, loose change, a small, unicorn-shaped black eraser, some pens, and Simon Critchley's comparatively tiny book on Wallace Stevens, *Things Merely Are*, and you have the contents of my bag as I hovered in wordless thought on the small stage of a B Line car as it lunged into a New England night.

The trolley made its way, at 8:30 in the evening on the last day of February, aboveground, leaving Kenmore Square and approaching the Boston University campus stops. I stood and held onto the ceiling railing. Several Japanese students sat just beneath me. On the same side of the trolley as these students but farther away from me, more towards the front of the car, two women in their mid-thirties, perhaps, but haggard, their hair long and bedraggled, sat side by side, propping each other up, obviously inebriated. They wore shapeless sweats and eye makeup. Occasionally they would speak loudly in drunken and metallic Boston accents. Everyone was ignoring them, but everyone knew they were there. Sitting in one of the single seats on the other side of the aisle, back closer to me, was a young man wearing a flat-brim baseball cap and a black-and-yellow Boston Bruins jersey. He occasionally eyed the two women with a not quite entirely concealed disdain. It was only a question of time, some of us seemed to know, before some sort of scene, probably mild, unfolded.

Behind the young man, in the other single seat, a young woman sat swipe texting on her phone, sliding her finger back and forth across the screen, from letter to letter, an orange tracer following her finger and creating rudimentary web-like patterns on the screen, a bit of technology I'd not yet seen before. Wherever her finger changed direction or made the least hesitation, a letter was produced, and words guessed by the phone, not suggested, or maybe even simply, intuitively completed, or completely intuited. I stood above her, too, and I could not help watching the orange webs form on the keyboard-screen as she composed missives in a rapid stream of finger slides. There was a significant blur between her humanity and her technology that seemed reflective of the murky distinction between reality and fiction. Were we *all* characters in a scene from *Infinite Jest*, left on the cutting room floor? Is it possible that a novel can suggest us to ourselves as if we were words that it might have made use of?

I have a brief and almost entirely undetectable role as an extra in *Infinite Jest*; I'm there insignificantly, a character on the furthest margins of the book, *outside* the margins, in fact, tiny, lost both above and within the letters and words of the book he's reading, experiencing nirvana again.

DFW and the Postmodern Novel of Ideas
Rob Short

> *Certain novels not only cry out for critical interpretations but actually try to direct them. [...] Frequently, too, those novels that direct their own critical reading concern themselves thematically with what we might consider highbrow or intellectual issues—stuff proper to art, engineering, antique lit., philosophy, etc. These novels carve out for themselves an interstice between flat-out fiction and a sort of weird cerebral roman à clef.*
>
> —David Foster Wallace, "The Empty Plenum: David Markson's *Wittgenstein's Mistress*"

Written while finishing his thesis in philosophy, Wallace's *The Broom of the System* ranks among other "novels of ideas" by philosophers like Sartre, Kierkegaard, or Camus. But shortly after *Broom* was published, Wallace read David Markson's novel *Wittgenstein's Mistress*. Feeling that Markson had completely eclipsed what he had tried to do with *Broom*, in 1990 Wallace published an effusive 23-page analysis of *Wittgenstein's Mistress* in *The Review of Contemporary Fiction* wherein he dismissed his own novel as "pretty dreadful" (218). Wallace's dissatisfaction with his fictional treatment of Wittgenstein's language-philosophy, especially given how Markson was able to bring it to life, was still fresh in Wallace's mind as he wrote his next novel.

In a little-known (or, at least, little-cited) 1996 interview with *Speak* magazine, just after the publication of *Infinite Jest*, Wallace describes how his writing approach had evolved since *Broom*: "Now, ten years later, I understand that people read for intellectual reasons and emotions. I'm interested in a marriage of the two. Before, I wanted to throw out the emotional in favor of the technical. Now, I would get rid of the technique to save the emotion" (41+).

This paper looks at a couple of examples in Wallace's second novel, *Infinite Jest*, where he revises and extends the idea content of *The Broom of the System*. It also proposes that Wallace's updated approach, his particular synthesis of intellect and emotion, constitutes a new category of writing, which category I will wincingly refer to as "The Postmodern Novel of Ideas" because that's what I called it in the abstract I submitted and am now stuck with for the purposes of at least this presentation because it's printed right there on the schedule.

A thorough examination of the structural and stylistic ways that Wallace accomplishes this fusion of intellect and emotion in his fiction after *Broom* is—lucky for you—well beyond my scope here, which is confined to one particular intersection of these two narrative categories in Wallace's first two novels. Specifically, my argument concerns the places where these novels' affective centers—their characters—intersect with their common theoretical or philosophical idea-content as Wallace understood it: Wittgenstein's conceptions of solipsism and of "meaning as use."

This is not a wholly original move. My approach is one that Adam Kelly described back in 2010 in his essay "David Foster Wallace: The Death of the Author and the Birth of a Discipline." Toward the end of the piece, Kelly describes what he sees as a collective shift in critics' use of theory to engage with or talk about Wallace's fiction. Instead of doing a "reading" of Wallace—a deconstructive reading, a postcolonial reading, what have you—Kelly writes that in 2009, the presenters at the first Wallace-themed conferences held in Liverpool and New York "demonstrated a pronounced tendency to utilise theory in a way that emphasized Wallace's own assimilation and response to it, with the often explicit assumption that Wallace was himself versed [in the works of major critical] figures and engaging in implicit dialogue with them in his fiction." I think that at this point this "assumption" is a pretty well-founded one, given what Wallace has said on the matter in various interviews and critical essays of his own, one of which is of particular interest to my argument here. It appears in David Lipsky's extended interview with Wallace, conducted during the last leg of the *Infinite Jest* book tour.

In it, Wallace explains the theoretical idea-content that *The Broom of the System*'s narrative structure is built on, saying that "[The] entire book is a conversation between Wittgenstein and Derrida, and presence versus absence. We have a cast of characters who are afraid their names don't denote, word and referent are united in absence, which means Derrida…" where he then unfortunately interrupts his own train of thought (35).

With *Broom*, because Wallace was motivated primarily by the desire to show off intellectually, building an entire novel on this theoretical chassis yielded a rather conventional novel of ideas—one that sacrifices character realization in the name of grinding its particular theoretical axe or dazzling readers with metafictional technique. By 1996, Wallace is on record all over the place—in audio interviews on NPR, in his essay on Markson's novel, and in various other print publications saying disparaging things about his first novel. Here he is again talking to David Lipsky, characterizing his reaction to his editor's proposed cuts to *Broom*:

> I had four hundred thousand pages of continental philosophy and lit theory in my head. And by God, I was going to use it to prove to him

that I was smarter than he was. [...] And so, as a result, for the rest of my life[,] I will see that book occasionally at signings. And I will realize I was arrogant, and missed a chance to make that book better. And hopefully I won't do it again" (Lipsky 35-6).

That *The Broom of the System* is the work of a hyperintelligent grad student is clear. But some of the ways it flattens the complexities and contradictions of Wittgenstein's language-philosophy for comic effect or rhetorical or formal showmanship prevent it from exploring Wittgenstein's themes with any real depth. Even Wallace's summation of the novel to David Lipsky in the quote from a minute ago dismisses the one aspect of the text's engagement with theory that isn't played entirely for laughs, which is the question of the degree to which our experience is constituted by language. In the novel, Lenore's character is convinced rather literally by her grandmother that "All that really exists of my life is what can be said about it" (*Broom* 119). Realizing that life is "circumscribed by language, Lenore feels not quite in control of her own existence" (James). But it is finally the *way*—the formal narrative devices—*Broom* transcribes philosophical problems into fictional ones that impresses the reader—not the treatment of the problems themselves, an impression of form rather than content. Caryn James similarly sums up the novel's strengths and weaknesses in her review:

> The heart of the novel, though, is its verbal extravagance and formal variations, reflecting Lenore's belief that language creates and imprisons her[.] What's the difference, Mr. Wallace seems to ask, between the real Lenore and the [...] version in [these] stories? And, by extension, what's the difference between the real-life reader and Lenore in *The Broom of the System*? Wallace aims to create his own language game, a fictional system in which "something's meaning is nothing more or less than its function." The philosophical underpinnings of his novel are too weak to support this, though. There is too much flat-footed satire of Self and Other, too much reliance on Philosophy 101.

Many readers and critics—myself included—find plenty to admire in Wallace's first novel, especially given the age of its author and the circumstances of its creation. And yet it is his second novel that is recognized as the major accomplishment and high-water mark of his fiction output. It's not entirely uncommon to hear someone say that a Wallace novel changed his or her life; I have yet to hear anyone say that novel was *The Broom of the System*. When compared with *Infinite Jest*, one is left feeling that the author of *The Broom of the System* wasn't so much writing to an imagined audience but rather performing in front of a mirror.

By his second novel, Wallace knows there's nothing emotionally engaging about philosophical abstraction without a narrative that resembles the reader's lived experience. He also understood that readers' empathy is predicated on this recognition of commonality—a relationship between the reader and a text that, as Wallace explains to Lipsky, has a lot to do with the writer's relationship to that text:

> I'm proud of [*Infinite Jest*.] In a way that for instance I'm *not* proud of *Broom of the System*. Which I think shows some talent, but was in many ways a fuck-off enterprise. It was written very quickly, rewritten sloppily, sound editorial suggestions were met with a seventeen-page letter about literary theory that was really a not-very-interesting way… really a way for me to avoid doing hard work. (34)

But during the process of writing his second novel, Wallace's thinking has shifted dramatically: "I think I work harder now. [...] I think when I was twenty-two or twenty-three, I pretty much thought every sentence that came off my pen was great. [...] I feel like this thing, this is a living thing. With whom, with which I have a relationship that needs to be tended. [T]hat I feel un-lonely working on" (32-34). This is the writer's side of the aforementioned synthesis of intellect and emotion.

We see an example of this synthesis toward the end of *Infinite Jest*. In the infantilizing American culture of the novel, many of its characters—finding no other viable coping models available—respond to the problem of solipsistic isolation with drug use and, eventually, addiction. But in the passage where the recovering addict Don Gately regains consciousness in the hospital, though he is suffering from severe trauma, we find him refusing pain medication. Wallace explains the recovering addict's difficult feat of restraint by letting us in on Gately's coping technique: "Abiding. No one single instant of it was unendurable. Here was a second right here: he endured it. What was undealable-with was the thought of all the instants all lined up and stretching ahead, glittering" (860). This technique is one that Gately learned during a forced detox in jail: "Gately remembered some evil fucking personal detoxes. [...] Feeling the edge of every second that went by. Taking it a second at a time. [...] Any one second: he remembered: the thought of feeling like he'd be feeling this second for 60 more of these seconds–he couldn't deal. He could not fucking deal. He had to build a wall around each second just to take it" (859-60).

Said another way: the period of his withdrawal, like the pain he's experiencing in the hospital, when conceptualized as a continuous, uninterrupted expanse of time, amounts to experiencing the entire aggregate effect of each moment simultaneously. Gately's solution is to *choose* to understand or idealize time as a series of static moments, separate from one another like the individual frames of a film reel. Paradoxically, during this exercise, Gately realizes that he had "never before or since felt so excruciatingly alive. Living in the Present between pulses. It's a gift, the Now: it's AA's real gift: it's no accident they call it *The Present*" (860). The phrasing of Gately's technique may sound familiar. Its source is taken from another theoretical work whose title is mentioned earlier in the narrative. The original formulation is from William James's *Gifford Lectures*, later published under the title *The Varieties of Religious Experience*, which along with his other genre-launching book, *Principles of Psychology*, established James as America's foremost philosopher and theoretician. A copy of James's *Gifford Lectures* and *Principles of Psychology* (as they're generally published now) appears earlier in the narrative. Its owner, Lenz, (one of the novel's models of how *not* to cope) has hollowed out its midsection to use as a cocaine stash.

But compare Gately's technique of conceptualizing time that he learned in A.A. to James's description of a religious adherent who has achieved a certain kind of inner peace:

> [She is] never anxious about the future, nor worr[ied] over the outcome of the day; [she] took cognizance of things, only as they were presented to her in succession, *moment by moment*. To her holy soul, the divine moment was the present moment, [...] and when the present moment was estimated in itself and in its relations, and when the duty that was involved in it was accomplished, it was permitted to pass away as if it had never been, and to give way to the facts and duties of the moment which came after. (317-18)

And Gately isn't the only character in this section of the novel to profess the usefulness of this divide-and-abide method of enduring otherwise unendurable stretches of time. Joelle van Dyne tells Gately that without a mindset capable of living in the present, she isn't surprised that her previous attempts at staying sober had failed:

> 'This was why I couldn't get off and stay off. Just as the cliché warns. I literally wasn't keeping it in the day. I was adding the clean days up in my head. [...] I'd throw away the pipe and shake my fist at the sky and say As God is my fucking witness NEVER AGAIN, as of this minute right here I QUIT FOR ALL TIME. [...] And I'd bunker up all white-knuckled and stay straight. And count the days. I was proud of each day I stayed off. [...] I'd add them up. Line them up end to end. You know? [...] And soon it would get...improbable. And the rest of the year, looking ahead, hundreds and hundreds [...] Who could do it? How did I ever think anyone could do it that way?' (859)

Another addict in *Infinite Jest*, Hal Incandenza, comes to a similar conclusion regarding his particular coping mechanism and its effect on how he experiences time: "It occurred to me that without some one-hitters to be able to look forward to smoking alone in the tunnel I was waking up every day feeling as though there was nothing in the day to anticipate or lend anything any meaning" (853).

Compared to the deployment of theory in *The Broom of the System*, *Infinite Jest*'s diffuse and subtle use of James's pragmatic theory as a response to Wittgenstein represents an order-of-magnitude jump in sophistication. *Broom*'s diegetic world distills the consequences of Wittgenstein's philosophy into a comically absurd joke with a glib punchline: "the truth is that there's no difference between a life and a story" (*Broom* 120). The latter novel spends 1,100 pages putting competing theoretical models into dialogue with one another in order to realize their cultural and psychic costs in lived human experience. *Infinite Jest* presents critical theory as an answer to the universally-human problem of enduring what we'd rather not, which allows for readers' identification with that theory through the affective channels of the novel's very different characters. Further, *Infinite Jest* is brimming with intertextual references—like the William James example above—that will repay the reader's time spent tracking them down with a deeper understanding of the novel; they are signposts to those philosophical and theoretical conversations the novel engages in or pushes back against. That these references convey additional meaning to *Infinite Jest*'s narrative—and most do—is another method of establishing a connection with readers through extratextual conversation.

Another comparison between the two novels I'd like to draw your attention to involves the way that *Infinite Jest* revises a specific narrative element it shares with *The Broom of the System*. Namely, a broom. First, here's the only passage where the word "broom" appears in the novel:

> Has she done the thing with the broom with you? [...] What she did with me [...] was to sit me down in the kitchen and take a straw broom and start furiously sweeping the floor, and she asked me which part of the broom was more elemental, more fundamental, in my opinion, the bristles or the handle. The bristles or the handle. And I hemmed and hawed, and she swept more and more violently, and I got nervous, and finally when I said I supposed the bristles, because you could after a fashion sweep without the handle, by just holding on to the bristles, but couldn't sweep with just the handle, she tackled me, and knocked me out of my chair, and yelled into my ear something like, "*Aha,* that's because you want to *sweep* with the broom, isn't it? It's because of what you want the broom *for,* isn't it?" Et cetera. And that if what we wanted a broom for was to break windows, then the *handle* was clearly the fundamental essence of the broom, and she illustrated with the kitchen window[...] but that if we wanted the broom to sweep with, see for example the broken glass [...] the bristles were the thing's essence. [...] Meaning as fundamentalness. Fundamentalness as use. Meaning as use. Meaning as use. (149-50)

So that's *Broom*'s broom. It functions as a rather ham-fisted example of one of Wittgenstein's language theories—just in case you didn't pick up on it in the quotation—it's that Wittgenstein wrote that meaning is determined by use.

If you've guessed where I'm going with the broom that appears in *Infinite Jest*, this next comparison may seem a little unfair, but stick with me. Let's compare the emotional pull of the preceding rapid-fire monologue in that preceding quotation from *Broom* with the only place in *Infinite Jest* that the word broom comes up (other than in the O.N.A.N. logo). I'll spare you a read-through of it for the sake of time and because it's possibly the most graphic depiction of violence I've ever encountered, but it's the scene where Lucien Antitoi is murdered in his and his brother's shop by a member of the wheelchair assassins. And for those of you who haven't read this or have read it and forgotten it, which I don't think is really possible: He's murdered with his own hand-carved broom. It's the most brutal violence in the novel, and Wallace chooses Lucien's own personal and well-loved broom as the murder weapon. And if this being (with the one exception I mentioned earlier) the only mention of a broom in *Infinite Jest* isn't coincidence enough to convince you that Wallace is drawing a deliberate parallel here, I should also mention that as Lucien is being impaled with the newly-sharpened point of his own broomstick, the wheelchair assassin who's doing the impaling has twice already, in the same sentence, used the French word for "useless" to describe Lucien's resistance to the A.F.R. before giving the word some particularly cruel emphasis when "the broom is shoved in and abruptly down by the big and collared A.F.R., thrust farther in, rhythmically, in strokes that accompany each syllable in the wearily repeated '*In-U-Tile*'" (488). Here, I think we have Wallace chastising his previous novel openly: Yes, meaning is use, but *what use one chooses* is a far more important point in one's day-to-day lived experience.

My last example concerns the formalistic choices Wallace made regarding the end of his two novels. In another passage from Lipsky's book, Wallace and Lipsky touch briefly on the distinction between more traditional, character-driven fiction and philosophical, idea-driven fiction in their own reading habits. Wallace tells Lipsky: "My tastes in reading lately have been way more realistic, because most experimental stuff is hellaciously unfun to read" (Lipsky 36). Equating the experimental with the novel of ideas, Lipsky asks: "*Because the ideas are primary? And the writing goes bad?*" Interestingly, Wallace explains his preference as a function of work: "I'm not sure if it's poorly written: It requires an amount of work on the part of the reader that's grotesquely disproportionate to its payoff." I think ultimately, this was the way Wallace had come to feel about *Broom*: That the amount of work it asked readers to put in was so disproportionate to the payoff it provided that the transaction between the writer and the reader basically amounted to one of bad faith. And at the heart of *Broom*'s inability to deliver readerly payoff was the way that theory functioned in the novel. So many of *Broom*'s characters function as little more than mouthpieces for theorists. Conversely, theory and theorists appear throughout *Infinite Jest*—from William James to Deconstruction to Deleuze & Guattari, but the way theory functions in the narrative is deliberately muted[1].

The Broom of the System notoriously ends mid-sentence—a move that Wallace's editor advised him against. And by the time of the Lipsky interview in 1996, Wallace has come to regard the ending as "a very cynical argument[.] There was a part of me [that] needed that ending[.] There was good stuff about it, but it was way too clever. It was all about the *head*. It's a brilliant little theoretical document—unfortunately it resulted in a shitty and dissatisfying ending" (Lipsky 35-36). In the *Speak* magazine interview I referenced in my opening, Wallace expands further on why he felt *Broom* had failed: "If you don't make fun of me, I'll tell you what I was trying to do. I was very interested in technical semantics, which is the relationship between form and context. That paragraph at the end [of *Broom*] is missing the word 'word,' so I thought I would bridge both the formal and the reference. Instead, I missed on both counts. [...]The ending that I wrote is almost off putting, like giving the finger to the reader" (Speak 41+).

Unlike his first, when Wallace's *second* novel concludes, what's left unsaid doesn't risk alienating readers so that it can get in one last metafictional wink. Rather, *Infinite Jest*'s ending leaves us with questions about the resolution of conflicts within the fictional world of the novel (What's happening to Hal in the opening scene? What's the ultimate fate of the master cartridge of the *Entertainment*? Am I supposed to read Orin's fate literally? How is Gately talking to the wraith of James Incandenza?)

This is because Wallace succeeds in making us care about what happens to his characters, succeeds in forging an actual connection with the reader. Furthermore, Wallace has dropped enough hints along the way to satisfy these narrative questions if we're reading closely—and this is finally the point: This is our portion of the work. This is our end of the conversation. And things like Infinite Summer and the wallace-l listserv attest to his success in getting us to do that work. This ratio of work vs. payoff is often cited by readers of *Infinite Jest*—both its detractors and admirers. For me, and I'd venture to guess for many of you, *Infinite Jest* succeeds precisely because the amount of work we put into reading it has been repaid not only in the traditional sense of reading enjoyment, but more importantly in extratextual ways, in the spheres of our day-to-day existence *outside* the text. This conference is one of them.

I call *Infinite Jest* a "postmodern novel of ideas" not because it swings the

---

1 Well, not all the time. There's that Eschaton section where Pemulis screams "It's snowing on the goddamn *map*, not the *territory*, you *dick*!" (333)

pendulum to the opposite extreme of the idea-driven vs. character-narrative driven continuum or because its mode is one of uncritical realism. It is what I think we can rightly call a "postmodern novel of ideas" in that it manages to resolve the unnecessary conflict between the character-novel vs. idea-novel binary by dismissing this distinction as a false choice; what Wallace says in my epigraph of *Wittgenstein's Mistress* can be applied to *Infinite Jest*: It should be numbered among those novels that "carve out for themselves an interstice between flat-out fiction and a sort of weird cerebral *roman à clef*"; and it embodies those things that such novels accomplish when they succeed:

> [T]hey serve the vital & vanishing function of reminding us of fiction's limitless possibilities for reach & grasp[,] for sanctifying the marriages of cerebration & emotion, abstraction & lived life, transcendent truth-seeking & daily schlepping, marriages that in our happy epoch of technical occlusion & entertainment-marketing seem increasing consummatable only in the imagination ("Empty Plenum" 218).

Infinite Jest is possessed of an affective register sufficient to evoke sincere readerly empathy for its characters while thoroughly and faithfully exploring the philosophical problems or theoretical questions which serve as its framework. However, one could say the same things about Markson's novel *Wittgenstein's Mistress*. (And for that matter, probably about Beckett's *How It Is* and Nabokov's *Pale Fire*.) Wallace's governing theoretical concern in *Infinite Jest* remains that of the problem of solipsism in Wittgenstein's language-philosophy. So what, if anything, about *Infinite Jest* sets it categorically apart?

Wallace accomplishes this distinction by creating characters who are clearly representations of competing or contradictory theoretical ideas, yet who are alive enough to engage us emotionally to the degree that we find ourselves speculating about what eventually happens to them after the narrative is over. *Infinite Jest* evolves beyond *Broom*'s simple ventriloquizing of Wittgenstein's theories into a maximalist narrative that dramatizes the logical consequences of those ideas in terms of real human cost: isolation, loneliness, depression, addiction. Additionally, what categorically separates *Infinite Jest* from *Wittgenstein's Mistress* is that it is not content to faithfully render some of the most poisonous aspects of our culture without offering some kind of antidote. Some of *Infinite Jest*'s characters enact workable human responses to the problems in Wittgenstein's philosophy that obsessed Wallace the most—those that he found it impossible to negate from within the conventions of a purely philosophical text. His postmodern novel of ideas allows his characters the narrative space to illustrate their effectiveness (or ineffectiveness) as curative strategies.

By showing us what happens to these characters, Wallace paradoxically *fictionalizes* these ideas in such a way that they are made *real* to us as readers, giving us the tools we need to narrow contemporary theory's crowded field competing of ideas by example. And this is Wallace's greatest gift to us as a writer: If you care for somebody, you don't do the work for them. You show them how to do it so that they can do it themselves. You run alongside them and hold them upright while they pedal frantically and wobble the handlebars, but eventually you stop running and pull away and watch them go.

Works Cited

James, Caryn. "Wittgenstein Is Dead and Living in Ohio." *New York Times* 1 Mar. 1987 late ed.: A22. Print.

James, William. *The Varieties of Religious Experience: A Study in Human Nature.* New York: Modern-Random, 1999. Print.

Kelly, Adam. "David Foster Wallace: The Death of the Author and the Birth of a Discipline." *Irish Journal of American Studies* 2 (2010). n. pag. Web. 6 Jan. 2015.

Lipsky, David. *Although Of Course You End Up Becoming Yourself: A Road Trip with David Foster Wallace.* New York: Broadway, 2010. Print.

Wallace, David Foster. *The Broom of the System.* New York: Viking, 1987. Print.

---. "The Empty Plenum: David Markson's *Wittgenstein's Mistress*." *Review of Contemporary Fiction* 10.3 (1990): 217-239. Print.

---. *Infinite Jest.* Boston: Little Brown, 1996. Print.

---. "1458 Words with David Foster Wallace." *Speak Magazine* Spring 1996: 41+-42+. Print.

Dog Stories
Jane L. Carman

Story 1: It is an honor to be the world's ugliest dog. Every year in California (the plastic surgery capital of the US), a contest is held that honors the world's ugliest dog's owner with a thousand dollars and a bag of publicity. Past winners of this prestigious award include Yoda, Pabst, Elwood, and three-time winner Sam (blindness a plus for Sam). While ugliness is as subjective as beauty, it can also be met with a bullet to the brain, a burlap sack and concrete block, or a simple twist of the neck. (Conversely, ugly girls are looked upon with pity whenever it is possible to look at them at all. The owners of ugly girls are never awarded a thousand dollars nor do they get any press at all for possessing such a creature.)

Story 2: Replacing a crow and a pair of geese, there is a dog sitting under a tree with a girl. She uses him as a pillow. She uses him as a friend, tells him stories about being called names that she does not understand. She is a dirty girl, the names say. A slut, they say. The dog listens, waiting for the hotdogs that will follow the sobbing. The dog listens, waiting for the girl to pull ticks, to brush his coat, to hold his muzzle in both hands and kiss his face with soft affection that travels down his spine until it reaches his tail and shakes his understanding of love and safety and sadness.

Story 3: Seventy dogs were seized from the property of a powerful League of Players star for evidence of dog fighting and animal abuse. Under the busted operation, those dogs who passed "training" to make them aggressive were allowed to live to fight. If fighting meant living. Those who refused to become aggressive enough to star in the sport selected for them were (inhumanely) destroyed. While one dog year equals seven human years of life, it is unclear how many dogs' lives are worth a single human life, as the defendant is back in the League of Players making public announcements against animal abuse and the sport of dog fighting.

Story 4: A dog loves the taste of lamb, is surrounded by small, soft-boned newborns. Their scent teasing his taste, traveling through his memory, his mouth watering. Dry processed kibble in his bowl freezing in the Midwestern February air. Dog fighting the memory of boots in ribs and the touch of human hands to love or discipline. Affection versus instinct. Processed imitation meat versus that thing he wants most. To satisfy a primordial urge to eat. To survive. To exercise his right to hunt. The scent of lanolin and milky breath and he can't take it any longer, drives his young teeth through the neck, blood flowing into his mouth. Swallowing life. He hurries to finish the carcass. Too late. There are rocks chucked at his head. He blacks out for a moment before returning to the boot that separates ribs. He slinks away, belly creating a trench in the snow. Later, he finds forgiveness, jumps into the cab of the pickup and rides to the top of the hill to a field waiting for spring. When the truck stops, he gets out to mark the field, to sniff for rabbits or squirrels. He feels a thud to the back of his head, drops to the ground, and sinks into the earth.

Story 5: A dog is a girl's best friend. If there is such a thing as a best friend or a dog.

Story 6: Either looking to have a good time or repulsed by the presence of a little lab, the puppy's owners begin to break legs one at a time. When the first leg snaps, the wailing of the pup swells. To control the noise, the mouth of the creature is glued shut, followed by the eyes and ears, just to make sure no sound escapes. After the final three limbs are broken, the still-living puppy becomes a liability. Knowing that there might be a fine or charges filed or that the body might die and begin emitting the stench of decomposition, the owners take the puppy to a nearby dumpster where it is tossed away and later dies.

Story 7: There are dogs that weave their way in and out of a life. They live and are murdered or die or escape the pull of a human life, always coming back and forth on tiny threads of that life working their way into dreams and actions and time. Resting only when the life spins in place. Reigning in rage and sorrow. Forcing terror out of the thick air surrounding (out)laws. Apparitions of love and tenderness, they cannot help but cycle and recycle through perception, waiting for it let go, waiting for it to reach for them and finally escape.

Story 8: A family visits a shelterand brings home a shepherd rescued from a puppy mill. The timid dog spends three months in the hands of gentle humans. Every day for three months she is groomed, stroked, nuzzled, fed, watered, and given boxes of treats. Her responses move from being paralyzed when touched to tail wagging and, eventually, to whining when her family leaves. After building a large fence to protect the dog and give her the opportunity to enjoy the great outdoors, the family leaves home long enough for the dog to be abducted. Her toenails are trimmed below the quick, each toe bleeding. Her teeth are filed almost to the gum line and she is placed on the soft grass of a freshly mowed lawn. She is introduced to a large male on a leash. Her abductor says things like, Sick em. And, Get er. And, Go. And, Fight. As the abductor boots her in the side a growl brews from deep within the large male morphing into a series of staccato barks. He lunges forward, teeth closing down on her muzzle, ripping away the freshly groomed fur. She cowers as teeth clench her neck. The abductor pulls back the large male, frees the bitch. She stands and begins to growl, nips at the male, her gums slipping away. The abductor frees the male to clench down on her neck once more, this time there is nothing or nobody to temper his rage.

Story 9: There are dogs who bark too loud, too often. They chase raccoons and squirrels and warn their owner of a pack of coyotes approaching the hen house. Every night there is a routine of barking and chasing and protecting, because this is what the owner expects and what the dogs are driven by nature to do. There are neighbors who are certain that the owner is herself a bitch, neighbors who dislike the sound of barking. There are cops who draw imaginary lines across property boundaries. There are neighbors who take things into their own hands with rifles and rat poison and heavy machinery. There are dogs who disappear and dogs who are captured and dogs who never barked but eat large doses of green pellets manufactured to make rodents slowly bleed to death.

Story 10: There is a dog. One that rides on the tank of a motorcycle. One that rides in the car of a young girl searching. One that is abandoned, given to a farm and a father figure or a mother lost in madness. One that disappears. One that climbs a fence, front legs holding down barbed wire, back legs stepping up each row of wire. Front legs struggling to reach the ground as barbs sink into stomach flesh and then the hide of the back legs and the front legs, reaching for the ground, reaching for the girl, reaching for the shelter of the shade tree where the tangled dog was once pillow and friend. Legs and emotion reaching. Barbs digging deeper, slicing skin, working their way into meat but not into anything vital like a heart or liver or soul. The dangling dog dangling waits for rescue or death. Barbs digging, prying open threads of meat. Just waiting. And nobody knows. Nobody cares. Nobody saves the dog, sun pushing hard against his dark coat. Tongue reaching for water. Memory reaching for time. And nobody knows. Nobody rescues the accidental dog until death slowly seeps in, shutting down one organ at a time. A kidney one day, a liver the next, until the heart can no longer work alone, until hope fails and there is nothing left but a carcass decaying in the autumn sun.

Story 11: Before Bob Barker wanted your pet spayed or neutered, there were dogs having puppies because that's what dogs did. The bitch had a litter of fourteen little brown coydogs, canines that would never make a pet, that would surely terrorize livestock and children. Thirteen of the puppies were tossed into a burlap sack and taken to the river where they floated and sunk and resurfaced, catfish biting on burlap until the sack came undone and the bodies freed to sink or wash up and decay. The fourteenth puppy was kept as an experiment. It learned to herd cattle, chase foxes and raccoons or opossums away from the chicken house, to comfort crying children or women (and men), and to sit, heal, and fetch a stick or ball.

Story 12: It is legal to shoot your own dog so long as it is not done in a manner that causes excessive suffering. It is legal to ask a vet to kill your dog via lethal injection, even if your dog is happy, healthy, and has not committed a crime nor been tried and convicted by a jury of its peers. It is illegal to shoot a girl, even if she is suffering, homely, or has a broken bone.

Story 13: A dog is man's best friend until time comes to pull the trigger.

"Dog Stories" was previously published in *580-Split* and in *Tangled in Motion* (Journal of Experimental Fiction Books, 2015).

Scattershot
Amy L. Eggert

In a flash of light off steel,
the boy turned into a man,
paralyzed at the threshold,
not yet thirteen,
his sweaty palm locked in
the girl's two-fisted grip.
She cowered in his shadow,
an ashen wraith in a My Little
Pony nightgown. Across
the room, their mother shrugged
against the stove, the blade
quivering in her hands, her
left eye puffed and purpling,
swollen from rage or a surprise
right hook. A stripe of red
straddled the Man's forearm,
droplets of blood drizzling
on kitchen tile.

The Man thundered something about forgiveness, something about
adverse effects of the medication, something about show some
fucking compassion, something about an exaggerated startle
response, something about snapping her neck like a twig.

The pair in the doorway ignored
or unseen, ghost children caught
in the periphery but lost
when given full attention.

The Man died dangling from attic rafters, a rope snaking ceiling-down, coiled around his neck.

When the boy was in grade
school, a neighborhood block
party exposed him to what
their mother called post-
traumatic stress disorder.
Purple popsicle juice melted
over his fingers as he watched
the Man flip over the snack
table when the high-schooler
next door set off the firecrackers.
Smaller kids snickered as parents
pulled them off to the side,
as corn cobs bounced off
the sidewalk, as potato salad
littered the lawn. The Man
huddled behind a card table,
color draining from his face,
tears streaming like a child's
from pinched shut eyes,
knees of his jeans stained red
in a puddle of punch.
Picnic trench warfare.

The Man lost his leg in a roadside bomb explosion in Iraq. In the same moment, he watched his friend blown apart, from the waist up: gone.

The boy would waken
to the sound of thunder.
In a window flash of lightning,
the Man would appear,
his silhouette black against
purple sky, his back to
the boy, staring inarticulate
out into the night. In the next
flash of light, the pane
would be empty, shade
framing drops of rain
splashing off the outside,

the boy wondering whether
he'd been dreaming, asleep.
Sometimes in the next room,
the Man's voice, the low-
pitched rumble of distant
gunfire.

The Man died mistaken as an intruder, a baseball bat to the skull.

The Man was a residual
haunt in the house, moving
as a shadow through hall
ways, walls, his daily routine.
Unaffected by those around
him, a storm passing through.
The night he returned, crownless
and on crutches, their mother
whispered something about chronic nightmares and flashbacks, a
bout clinical depression, about patience, leeway, the need for space.

The highs of combat
were unattainable in civilian
life, so the Man sought them
in what others deemed reckless
behavior, in bar brawls and
bottles of scotch discarded
in bulk in the garage, under
the kitchen table, on the back
porch, in the purr of his black
Honda Shadow Spirit.

The popping, snapping of cartilage, of tendons letting go,
the splintering of bone. The Man knew his leg was gone
as soon as the shrapnel chewed into his flesh.

The Man died flying back into battle, the engine sputtering, failing,
a shining speck in the sky, plunging.

The girl's adolescence
was marred by pink tufts
of insulation wafting,

recollections of kitchen
knives glinting in the light,
blood trickling onto tile,
her fear reflected in their
mother's eyes, and
hopscotch on the rocks
paper scissor.
She sank.
The boy's own strange
and phantom fury matured
alongside stacked firewood
and slurred accusations.

Something about that girl shows no respect, something about teach
your goddamn kids some goddamn manners, something about
don't make me take matters into my own hands, 'cuz so help
me god I'll do it.

The girl came home one
morning, a baby inside, left
with a split lip and their mother,
came home again, a stitched lip,
the baby gone.

The Man lost his leg to a motorcycle accident between tours, asphalt
tearing, ravaging his flesh like shrapnel. The popping, snapping,
letting go. The splintering of bone.

The Man died at seventeen, crossing the street toward an arcade,
drunken high beams swerving.

The boy was the ghost
in the house, the phantom
warrior turning furious,
the fear of turning into the Man,
rage scaling his throat like bile,
too acidic to contain, white
phosphorous daydreams
of his father, the Man,
towering over the mangled
faces of disfigured children,

their bulbous features rotting
off in hospitals where injured
soldiers cried for their mothers.

The Man died at 86, a leg lost to diabetes, heart stuttering, failing.

Their mother screamed at the Man
once, charged him with being
insensitive, inaccessible,
abusive, abrasive, amputated
from her, from their children,
from responsibility, from reality.

The Man snatched his shotgun
from its dusty mount on the wall.
Drunk on adrenaline, on scotch
on the rocks, on antidepressants,
on blue sleeping pills, bombed
out of his mind, out of his left
boot, his buddy blown in half,
he warned her to back off,
to stand down, or he'd blast her
head off, he swore to god.
Still she charged, her voice
the shrill siren of an inbound
air raid.

The girl's hands over her ears,
the boy wrested the 12 gauge
from the Man's grip, wrestled
him to the floor, but not before
shells exploded at close range,
insulation snowing down
from the ceiling, pink confetti
flecking the family room carpet,
ears left ringing, a jagged drywall
patch, a painted-over scar,
a reminder, a token, a souvenir
from battle on the home front.

The Man died in a pool of blood and body parts, debris on a dusty
street in Fallujah.

The Man often disappeared
in the middle of the night
in a flash of lightning
through bedroom curtains,
in a fluorescent wink off
a steel blade, in the chink
of ice on glass, in a motorcycle
snarl. Most mornings he
returned, hobbling on
a hangover or a prosthetic leg;
on others, at the kitchen
counter, their mother nursed
a cup of coffee, black, sipping
slowly, watching the back door,
listening for the distant wail
of sirens or tires screaming
over wet blacktop, waiting
for the apologetic knock
of tragic news brought by
the pair of disheartened
though stoic police officers
who hated this part of the job
until finally splashing the cold
remnants into the sink, retreating
to the back corners of the house
in silence.

Sometimes before the shower
shut off, the boy could hear
through his bedroom wall
their mother weeping beneath
the white noise of water
hitting her.

The Man lost his leg to a drunk driver as a teenager and even into his fifties complained of phantom limb pain, sensations of tingling, itching, burning, aching in his missing left ankle.

Before pink flurries
and threshold paralysis

transformed the boy phantom
furious, he climbed attic stairs
in search of tangled strands
of Christmas lights, found
instead the Man, his throat
bruising purple inside a knotted
noose, lips trembling in dread
or prayer, his eyes wide
and afraid. The boy cut the rope
loose with a slip joint pocketknife,
held his father's hand as the Man
inched rung by rung back down
off the ladder. Together they
strung the flashing colored bulbs
along the gutter.

The Man died in the road, flesh fused to metal and asphalt.

One chilled afternoon, the Man
chopped, the boy stacked
firewood. The sky, the lawn
decorated with the red and orange
and gold of autumn leaves.
They worked in the backyard
where the Man had taught
the boy how to balance the log
and arc the ax, how to watch
the ball and swing the bat
parallel to the ground while
the girl stooped nearby,
scrawling purple hearts
and hopscotch squares
with sidewalk chalk onto
the concrete patio slab.
The boy steadied a branch
between gloved hands, cracked
it in two.

The sudden fracture of wood,
the unexpected rupture of grain,
the family tree: the splintering

of bone, the concussion of riflefire,
the snapping of a wife's neck.
The Man turned on his son,
ax suspended over his head.

Leaves unleashed, letting go
of the trees, floating wearily
from the sky, bloody, like scraps
of heaven falling, like drops
of blood raining to kitchen tile,
like tufts of pink dropping
from holes in the family
room ceiling, like snow.

The Man died mangled on the kitchen floor, blood spreading black
beneath him on the tile.

The visitation was closed
casket so as not to showcase
the rope burns, the purple
shrapnel scars, the third degree
road rash, the dented forehead.
The Man's flag-draped coffin,
the organ prelude, the candlelit
shadowflickers against stained
glass, the boy's somber
and straight-faced eulogy,
the girl clutching to their mother,
the soldiers' 21 gun scotch shot
salute, the folding over of striped
and starred cloth, the sinking
of the Man's remains into soft
earth, the quiet retreat of three
home to a haunted house.

Listening for limped footfalls
on concrete outside, the chill
of aluminum in a sweaty palm,
the boy was the specter unseen,
the shadowed sentinel behind
the refrigerator, waiting.

The Man's staggered entrance,
keys fumbling, cursing inarticulate
under whiskey breath, his sword
of Damocles in the guise
of a baseball bat
locked in the boy's two-
fisted grip.

"Scattershot" was previously published in *Scattershot: Collected Fictions* (Lit Fest Press, 2015).

"Not Another Word":
Choice and Connection in *Infinite Jest*
Carissa Kampmeier

There are characters in *Infinite Jest* and *The Pale King* who are almost superhuman in their ability to transcend some of the problems of contemporary culture that David Foster Wallace is so adept at writing about—how hard it is to step outside yourself and really identify with another person from a place that isn't just self-serving, how difficult it is to pay attention to something, especially when that thing is boring. Mario Incandenza from *Infinite Jest* and Shane Drinion from *The Pale King* both have these kinds of superhuman abilities. Mario is especially capable of empathy, and Drinion can pay attention to anything. The problem is that these characters don't seem especially redemptive, at least not in a way that's helpful to us. We can't hope to be like them because empathizing and paying attention aren't difficult for them the way they are for everyone else. As Wallace calls it in "This Is Water," these are their "default settings" ("This Is Water"). I began examining what it means to be redeemed if you're a character in a Wallace novel and why characters that I originally thought of as a "way out" of solipsism and loneliness really weren't. In part, this arises from Mary K. Holland's charges in *Succeeding Postmodernism* that "every character in *Infinite Jest* who struggles against a culture of narcissism... suffers both emotionally and physically" and that "even earnest attempts to escape only lead back to new manifestations of the solipsistic loop" (74, 77). I will argue that Wallace gives us the key to understanding two of his major texts with "This is Water" and that examining characters from *Infinite Jest* and *The Pale King* through the lens of the Kenyon College commencement speech may help shape and broaden our understandings of what redemption might mean within these texts.

Mario Incandenza, whose physical disabilities are described in detail within *Infinite Jest*, also has an innate naïveté that makes him easy to connect with. He's described as a "born listener," and Wallace points out early on that one of the reasons ETA residents are so comfortable talking to Mario is a side effect of his disability (*Infinite Jest* 79-80). He writes, "One of the positives to being visibly damaged is that people can sometimes forget you're there, even when they're interfacing with you" (Wallace, *Infinite Jest* 80). Arguably, Mario's relationship with Hal is one of the most important in the novel. Each brother protects, and in some ways, even reveres the other. Wallace writes that "his younger and way more externally impressive brother Hal almost idealizes Mario, secretly. God-type issues aside, Mario is a (semi-) walking miracle, Hal believes" (*Infinite Jest* 316). It's Mario who gives Hal his first copy of the O.E.D., and it's Hal who chases the U.H.I.D. representative off the academy's driveway with a tennis racket (Wallace, *Infinite Jest* 317). One of Mario's greatest talents is the ability to treat others as though they're actually human. In the short anecdote about Clipperton, the suicidal tennis player, Mario is the only one who befriends him, and when Clipperton ultimately shoots himself, it's Mario who insists on cleaning the room afterward, a gesture that "took the bradykinetic Mario all night and two bottles of Ajax Plus to clean the room with his tiny contracted arms and square feet" (Wallace, *Infinite Jest* 433). It is also Mario who rescues the bum-in-disguise Barry Loach from the Boston Commons merely by being the only person to reach out and shake his hand and "extend some basic human warmth and contact" (Wallace, *Infinite Jest* 969). Mario's talent for real empathy seems innate rather than learned; i.e., it is not presented as a solution to solipsism or irony because there's no way to take it up. Wallace seems to be imagining a place where irony and loneliness are defeated, but such a place is inaccessible to most. The character who is most able to be empathetic is portrayed as, somehow, not quite human. For Mario, empathy is not a choice; it's his default setting.

With that in mind, it's not clear whether Mario's brand of empathy and human connection counts as redemptive. It's a real connection because he's a real person; I don't want to deny him that agency as a character, but like the interactions with television that Wallace describes in "E Unibus Pluram," relationships with Mario seem curiously lopsided; he is capable of giving without receiving. He asks so little from those around him that it's like a relationship without any of the risks. After Hal admits to hiding his marijuana habit from Mario, who reports being "zero percent hurt" by the secret, a frustrated Hal asks him to "be a fucking human *being* for once, Boo . . . Jesus it's like talking to a big poster of some smiley-faced guy" (Wallace, *Infinite Jest* 784). The smiley face is a sinister recurrence throughout the novel, etched onto copies of the fatal film cartridge and worn by members of the wheelchair assassins, and its association with Mario isn't clear. There is nothing sinister about Mario, but there is something curiously blank about him. He's incapable of being embarrassed or offended, which only adds to the sort of unreal quality of his character. It's as though, in this conversation, Hal wants to be held responsible for his secret-keeping, but Mario, like Avril with her hands-off, no-blame parenting style, simply cannot provide that. In the Larry McCaffery interview, Wallace refers to absolute freedom as "deadening" and, in the novel, it is often an agent of destruction (McCaffery, "An Expanded

Interview" 52). Relationships with Mario and Avril, which are equally free and without limits, may be just as destructive. It's possible that the smiley face mask is associated with Mario because he represents another dead end. Despite his capability for empathy, connection with him, like with the deadly entertainment cartridge, is not a way out. Empathy alone is not enough to escape a deeply flawed and narcissistic culture.

Like *Jest*, there is one character in *The Pale King* who transcends the problems that are foregrounded in the rest of the characters. Shane Drinion has an almost superhuman ability to pay attention to anything without the enormous difficulty or the kind of "psychic pain" that characters like David Cusk and Lane Dean suffer (Wallace, *Pale King* 87). Anything he pays close attention to becomes almost magically interesting to him, to the point where he actually "levitates slightly" when he experiences total immersion (Wallace, *Pale King* 487). However, it's not clear that, toward the end of the novel, Drinion and Meredith are actually connecting as she tells him the story of how she met her husband. There's no sense of empathy with him; it's like grasping the syntax of a sentence but not the meaning. Again, Wallace seems to be searching for places where the problems of being a human are transcended, but they're not without complications, and they're not really presented as solutions. Empathy and paying attention are default settings for these characters, but empathy and attention alone don't seem like enough to make the kinds of human connections that might be a real escape from solipsism.

In spite of this difficulty, we see characters in *Infinite Jest* actively trying to make meaningful connections, and some actively trying (or pretending to try) and failing. It's the very premise of AA meetings, where members are encouraged to really listen and try to identify with one another's stories. In a conversation at a bar with Remy Marathe, Kate Gompert remarks, "I'm Identifying every step of the way with you, Ramy. Oh *God*, what did I *say*" (Wallace, *Infinite Jest* 777). Like Wallace, Kate can't help but acknowledge the banality of empathizing (and she's so tipsy she gets Marathe's name wrong), but less than a page later, she reiterates, "I am so totally Identifying it's not even *funny*" (Wallace, *Infinite Jest* 777). These ironic parodies of attempts to Identify are contrasted with Gately's earnest efforts at AA meetings. He reflects:

> The residents' House counselors suggest that they sit right up at the front of the hall where they can see the pores in the speaker's nose and try to Identify instead of Compare. Again, *Identify* means empathize. Identifying, unless you've got a stake in Comparing, isn't very hard to do, here. Because if you sit up front and listen hard, all the speakers' stories of decline and fall and surrender are basically alike, and like your own. (Wallace, *Infinite Jest* 345)

The attention here is not on how all the stories are alike, which reduces empathy to simple narcissism, but on the genuine effort it takes to first, really listen to someone, and second, not see oneself as the single protagonist in some big, sad tragedy. This is hardly the usual, as many of the newer AA speakers fall prey to various mistakes, such as "performing" their narratives or trying to place blame. Gately reflects on the place as an "irony-free zone" (Wallace, *Infinite Jest* 369). Irony keeps the speakers from connecting, both with other addicts and with the real sources of their addictions.

Joelle's progress echoes Gately's, although comparatively, she's clean for much less time in the novel. In her earliest days at Ennet house, she reports feeling "pretty much cynical and repelled" by the meetings and their appeals to clichés, Higher Powers, and Identification (Wallace, *Infinite Jest* 361). She's a prime example of the kind of addict who has the hardest time recovering in the novel because of her tendency to intellectualize. Like ironizing, intellectualizing AA is actually detrimental to recovery, since it gets in the way of the ability to truly identify. Later in the novel, Joelle realizes that she's managed to stop overthinking everything at meetings. Listening to a speaker relate his addiction story, she reflects, "His story's full of colored idioms and those annoying little colored hand-motions and gestures, but to Joelle it doesn't seem like she cares that much anymore. She can Identify. The truth has some kind of irresistible unconscious attraction at meetings, no matter what the color or fellowship" (Wallace, *Infinite Jest* 708). This moment is not without mediation. Even as she claims to be empathizing, Joelle can't help noticing and characterizing his ticks as "colored," which, much like Kate Gompert's misuse of Marathe's name, may serve to undermine the whole moment, at least from a reader's perspective. Like his calling for "woodwinds" in the McCaffery interview, Wallace cannot quite escape the pull to be ironic in the midst of an attempt to say something real (McCaffery, "An Expanded Interview" 50). Joelle's effort seems sincere, but even sincere efforts are problematized. She's no less ironic by the end of the novel, but there are moments when she's able to suspend that reductive approach and make an effort to connect. Identifying with another human being is an active struggle since, as Wallace notes in his commencement speech, self-centeredness is our "default setting" ("This Is Water"). He remarks that "everything in my own immediate experience supports my deep belief that I am the absolute center of the universe; the realest, most vivid and important person in existence" (Wallace, "This Is Water"). Trying to get outside of this kind of thinking is one of the major themes of a lot of Wallace's fiction and some of his nonfiction, and it's the premise of the AA meetings, where residents are basically asked to try to connect with something outside themselves.

Connections that do happen in the novel, like Gately and Joelle's, are difficult to pinpoint. It's tentative but unacknowledged during the climactic scene where Gately is shot and suddenly recognizes her as Madame Psychosis, and later in the hospital when he's intubated and conscious of making "barnyard sounds" at her and embarrassing himself (Wallace, *Infinite Jest* 855). More obviously, Joelle reflects briefly on their relationship during the scene where she first realizes she is able to Identify with an AA speaker without being critical. She muses that "it's the first time she's felt sure she wants to keep straight no matter what it means facing. No matter if Don Gately takes Demerol or goes to jail or rejects her if she can't show him the face. It's the first time in a long time—tonight, 11/14—Joelle's even considered possibly showing somebody the face" (Wallace, *Infinite Jest* 710). This is a major development for her, since Joelle wears a U.H.I.D. veil specifically to hide her deformity. This connection doesn't "save" or reward either character, and it's not a cure-all for the very real problems they face in staying substance-free. In fact, there is in inherent risk in forming relationships with newly recovered addicts because of the tendency to displace responsibility.

It might be helpful here to think about what counts as redemptive in a novel. If the characters are "saved" or things are better for them by the end, then Mary Holland is right, and this is a very dark book indeed. Characters like Gately who try to make connections are only punished for it. But that may be where the message of "This is Water" becomes really important. We may never find in a Wallace novel a relationship that's uncomplicated or a relationship that solves problems for characters; it wouldn't be realistic, and Wallace fought to present in his fiction the world as he experienced and understood it. However, characters like Gately, and on a smaller scale, Joelle, who make genuine efforts to make connections, to escape solipsism and addiction seem to have something redemptive about them. That empathy has the power to help keep them off their Substances. Characters who do not make those attempts or maybe don't make them in the right ways suffer even more. Hal's failure to connect with others leads to an actual physical inability to communicate; at the chronological end of the novel he is, as Stephen J. Burn writes, "isolated in the loneliness of his own talent" (*David Foster Wallace's* Infinite Jest 25).

"This Is Water" reminds us that it is a decision, ultimately, to choose to alter our default thinking settings and make them less self-centered. I want to close with a discussion of a moment that I think best exemplifies what *Infinite Jest* is striving for and what *The Pale King*, in its existing text, only alludes to. I hope to argue that it's one of few proposed solutions to these problems of attention, language, and human connection in Wallace's fiction. In the short story "Good Old Neon," Wallace weaves an intricate mental monologue from the ghost of a recent suicide. In its final paragraphs, the narrative circles back to the author-as-character, David Foster Wallace sitting at his desk, remembering a high school acquaintance who recently committed suicide, and trying to imagine what might have driven him to such a conclusion. Again, we can see the impulse to over-analyze as Wallace-as-character starts to mentally berate himself over how impossible it is to ever know what it's like to be another human being (and the absolute narcissism of thinking that we can), when he suddenly stops himself, writing, "The realer, more enduring and sentimental part of him commanding that the other part be silent as if looking it levelly in the eye and saying, almost aloud, 'Not another word'" (Wallace, *Oblivion* 181). It's a brief moment where Wallace manages, out of what seems like sheer willpower, to escape the intellectual, solipsistic cycle that recurs throughout much of his writing. Wallace-as-character makes a conscious choice to turn off the part of his brain that intellectualizes to the point of paralysis. When Joelle is Identifying with a speaker at the meeting, she "chooses consciously to believe it isn't affected, the story's emotive drama" (Wallace, *Infinite Jest* 710). The emphasis is that it's a conscious choice, it is unbelievably difficult, it often fails, and as Wallace points out, "some days you won't be able to do it, or you just flat out won't want to" ("This Is Water"). His work suggests that any solution will be mediated and problematic, and that empathy and attention alone are not a cure-all for a culture that makes it increasingly hard to be human. But it also suggests that it's the conscious choice to try that matters, and that it is trying more than succeeding that has the power to affect real change. If there are moments of redemption in Wallace's fiction, they might look something like that.

Works Cited

Burn, Stephen J. *David Foster Wallace's Infinite Jest: A Reader's Guide*. 2nd ed. 2012. New York: Bloomsbury, 2013. Print.

Holland, Mary K. *Succeeding Postmodernism: Language and Humanism in Contemporary American Literature*. 2013. New York: Bloomsbury, 2014. Print.

McCaffery, Larry. "An Expanded Interview with David Foster Wallace." *Conversations with David Foster Wallace*. Ed. Stephen J. Burn. Jackson: UP of Mississippi, 2012. 21-52. Print. Literary Conversations Ser.

Wallace, David Foster. "E Unibus Pluram: Television and U.S. Fiction." *Review of Contemporary Fiction* 13.2 (1993): 151-94. Web.

---. *Infinite Jest*. 1996. New York: Back Bay, 2006. Print.

---. *Oblivion*. 2004. New York: Back Bay, 2005. Print.

---. *The Pale King*. 2012. New York: Back Bay, 2011. Print.

---. "This Is Water." Kenyon College. Gambier, OH. 21 May 2005. Commencement Speech. Web. 11 Dec. 2014.

"E Unibus Pluram"—A Postscript: Applying Social Networking to David Foster Wallace's Ideas Concerning Television and the Corrosive Effects of Irony

Jeff Jarot

In his essay "E Unibus Pluram," David Foster Wallace comments on the addictive nature of television, specifically the tendency of a particular "subspecies" of lonely human being to gaze longingly at the actions of a fascinating "Other" via a one-way television screen. Wallace insists that such gazers "love to watch people but hate to be watched [themselves]" (Wallace 22). Few would dispute that his arguments were cogent in 1993, the year his essay was first published, and they mostly remain so. Nevertheless, given the speed with which technology has advanced in the years since, one wonders what Wallace would have made of the game-changing metastasis of social-networking in present-day society. The writer passed away in 2008, three years after the virtual birth and cultural proliferation of Facebook.

Indeed, as was the case with television, the Internet and social-networking have been woven into the fabric of culture and society so thoroughly (and so speedily in the case of the latter two media) that their influence, especially its negative aspects, has been dismissed or, at the very least, downplayed. To borrow Wallace's 1993 words in relation to TV's less-than-positive influence, "we don't take [the Internet and social-networking] seriously enough as both a disseminator and a definer of the cultural atmosphere we breathe and process, that many of us are so blinded by constant exposure that we regard [them] the way Reagan's lame F.C.C. chairman Mark Fowler professed to see [TV] in 1981, as 'just another appliance, a toaster with pictures'" (Wallace 27).

In his 1993 essay Wallace argues that television viewers "are allergic to people" (Wallace 22). The same can be said of social-networkers, as long as such an accusation involves *real, actual* people and not *virtual* people. In reality, Facebook and sites of like ilk have created and propagated the illusion that their users need not fear of *ever* being alone. No longer do they have to carry the shameful albatross of solitary voyeurism around their necks. This is because social networks by their very nature require their subscribers to create their own individualized, personalized worlds, whose landscapes consist of an equal mix of personally selected words and photographs. These landscapes are narrated by carefully-composed prose, words whose sequences can be crafted to perfection, and only then is it necessary for the God-author to click on the "Post" button. Even then, if said prose is deemed to be the slightest shred imperfect, the "Edit" function can be employed. The result is a bizarre hybrid of the "real" (albeit mediated and meticulously constructed) visuals of "real" events that are nonetheless part of a similarly arranged narrative via related captions and posts. More than television has been able to do, not only does social networking allow people to access "what we as Audience want to see ourselves as" (Wallace 22), it offers us, as well as Wallace's coined Everyman, "Joe Briefcase," the opportunity to be our own Geppetos, the virtual woodcarvers of our own homegrown pruned and maintained virtual personas. Moreover, such self-created "virtual worlds" are malleable, ever-changing. One can mold her own Facebook page like clay, sculpting a work of art that will, gloriously, never be finished; it is always "in-progress." What this amounts to is that, like Wallace's television did before, social-networking "purveys and enables *dreams*" (Wallace 39) and allows for the creation of a "dream-self." For Wallace's Joe Briefcase, "true actualization of self would actually consist [of his] becoming one of the images that are the objects of this great herd-like watching" (Wallace 56). For countless social-network surfers, it is better to be trapped within the artificial-yet-pleasing, safer, more self-contained confines of Facebook than it is to deal with the trials and disappointments that our "real" selves face in the actual physical world.

Yet another revolutionary aspect of social media's virtually-paved street is that it offers lanes of communication in both directions. As is the case with those of whom Wallace writes in his 1993 essay, "the people we're watching through TV's framed-glass screen are not really ignorant of the fact that somebody is watching them" (Wallace 23). However, with social networking, TV's one-way mirror melts and evaporates, and in its place a two-way mirror forms, one to which, to the comfort and delight of Wallace's "loners," other viewers are invited, encouraged to test the virtual waters with their toes and walk the artificial beach, gazing around at their fellow "loners" and their self-created shores. In "E Unibus Pluram," Wallace suggests that "[if w]e spend enough time watching, pretty soon we start watching ourselves watching. Pretty soon we start to 'feel' ourselves feeling, yearn to experience 'experience'" (Wallace 34). Nowhere is this truer than on a social network.

Nevertheless, social-networking *does* retain a certain degree of one-way voyeurism in the sense that, although subscribers certainly long for others to view their carefully-crafted content with admiration, they can never be fully sure of *absolutely everyone* who is visiting their pages and is not leaving hand-and/or fingerprints in the form of posts and responses to posts. Despite this, like Wallace's TV, social networks involve "performance, spectacle, which by definition requires watchers" (Wallace 23). It inherently needs real lifeblood in the form of viewers, creators, participators, and voyeurs in order to exist. Our "friends" on Facebook are not dissimilar to Wallace's TV-spawned "networks of strangers connected by self-interest and technology" who similarly "offer us familiarity, community. Intimate friendship" (Wallace 26). Joe Briefcase, as was the case with his previous membership in the television-viewing community, experiences "inclusion in some attractive community," wherein "all [are] united as Happy Group" (Wallace 55). Wallace further argues in "E Unibus Pluram" that "people are always most vulnerable, hence frightened, hence persuadable, when they are approached solo" (Wallace 55). I would go one step further and ask: What *is* social-networking if *not* a solo act, sitting alone at a computer, tablet, or phone, interfacing with like-minded Others? Like the TV-viewing populace for which Wallace argues, "[t]he [social-networking] crowd is now paradoxically both (1) the 'herd' in contrast to which the viewer's distinctive identity is to be defined and (2) the witnesses whose sight alone can confer distinctive identity" (Wallace 56). Later on in his 1993 essay, Wallace suggests that "[t]he well-trained [television] viewer becomes even more allergic to people. Lonelier" (Wallace 63). Again I pose the question: How is all this different from the ever-growing herds of Facebook "friends?" The same arguments can be made for the lonely legions of social-networkers lounging in front of solitary screens, regardless of the platform.

Certainly, many people who have frequented social-networking sites can relate to either the rush and exhilaration or the despair and depression of being watched and followed and read (or not), for frequenters of social-networking sites desperately want us there to view, to witness, to appreciate their handiwork, and many become despondent when the fruits of their labor remain unplucked on the virtual tree. Everything, and I mean absolutely, positively everything—every picture posted, every typed thought shared, every load of laundry lauded, every photo of a meal drooled over before being hastily consumed, every faux fig on the virtual tree, is created self-consciously, shared for the sole purpose of itself being consumed, appreciated, fawned over, and of paramount importance, *liked*. Not a single person on Facebook or Twitter or wherever, *doesn't* want to be observed, feasted upon, followed, appreciated on as many computer screens, tablets, and phones as is humanly possible.

In present-day culture, like Wallace's television, "[w]e literally cannot imagine life without it" (Wallace 43), "it" being the Internet. With this in mind, Wallace further states that "a world we now view as constructed and not depicted becomes the medium that constructs our world-view" (Wallace 62). Moreover, what social-networking provides is the latest iteration of "meta-reality," where subscribers are self-consciously aware of the personalized, individualized versions of virtual reality they are molding.

Writer Shea Bennett, a self-proclaimed "Twitter expert," wrote recently that, according to a Cowen Company poll, social-networkers across all age groups spend an average of 42.1 minutes a day on Facebook, with younger subscribers spending marginally more time, 51 minutes, on the social network service. (Bennett 1) This is dwarfed by Wallace's 1993 assertion that "television is watched over six hours a day in the average American household" (Wallace 22). Could it be that Bennett's numbers are inaccurate and/or skewed? Perhaps they are low because nowadays there is a preponderance of choices with regard to how people settle on whiling away their time in comparison to the world of 1993, in which TV had a monopoly with regard to free time devoted to entertainment. Nevertheless, especially given the present portability of platforms and their near-ubiquity, audience members in this very room may very well be checking out their preferred social networks, perhaps even as I speak these very words *right now*!

For better or worse, the concepts of "object" and "place" are evaporating at a faster and faster rate in the present era. Physical books and albums and movies, along with the brick-and-mortar outlets where in years past consumers would purchase said physical products, have long since been supplanted on the whole by their ethereal, ephemeral, computer-birthed equivalents. However, the honking-huge white elephant in the room related to social-networking sites such as Facebook is that they are purported to be tools and venues through which we as subscribers are able to keep track of others, to *share* a sense of community, both in the old-school sense as well as the relatively newly-coined Facebook sense. However, social networks mainly function as solipsistic platforms on which we collectively are shamelessly promoting *ourselves*. In sum, all of this "sharing" is blatantly *an act*.

Of course, there is an added danger in all of this, which Wallace forewarns us of in "E Unibus Pluram."

> [P]suedorelationships...[become] acceptable alternatives to relationships with real people. [O]ne will have commensurately less incentive even to try to connect with real 3-D persons, connections that seem pretty important to basic mental health. For Joe Briefcase, as for many addicts, the special Treat begins to substitute for something nourishing and needed, and the original genuine hunger—less satisfied than bludgeoned—subsides to a strange objectless unease. (Wallace 38-9)

Furthermore, Wallace declares that "people in the same room don't do all that much direct conversation with each other" (Wallace 44), predicting the prevalent silences that result when people congregate in the present day only to keep their mouths closed, eyes transfixed on a screen, and thumbs manipulating keys that navigate the virtual pathways of a social-networking site. He goes on to say that "[i]t's not paranoid or hysterical to acknowledge that television [or, I posit, the Internet and social-networking] in enormous doses affects people's value and self-perception in deep ways" (Wallace 53).

Now, lest I come across as a preachy, finger-wagging boob who stands atop his soapbox and judges others indiscriminately, let it be known that I stand before you all in the waist-deep waters of the social-networking sea *guilty as charged. Disclaimer alert: I fully, openly, and slightly abashedly acknowledge my own hypocrisy.* I have had and most assuredly will continue to have my own bouts of social-networking addiction. Furthermore, it would be absolutely remiss of me not to concede that social networking, like the television that Wallace alternately rails against and embraces, provides, in his very words, "both *medicine* and poison" (Wallace 26). To not acknowledge the benefits of social-networking would amount to declaring myself a disciple of "anti-social-networking paranoia" (to pilfer in part a phrase of Wallace's). The benefits of social-networking certainly abound, a significant advantage being that it allows for the possibility of reconnecting with others whose previous, frequent correspondence has been lost for any number of reasons. Moreover, scholarly research, notwithstanding the need to carefully parse sources for credibility, has become blessedly easier and more efficient.

I suppose an old, crusty adage would be appropriate here, something along the lines of "devouring too much of something initially good becomes inherently bad." I certainly would not say that with regard to the present case of social-networking, "excess leads to" William Blake's "palace of wisdom." Rather, I think it simply has the dangerous potential to lead to a toxic form of more excess. Wallace says as much himself with regard to television, declaring, "We are responsible basically because nobody is holding any weapons on us forcing us to spend amounts of time second only to sleep doing something that is, when you come right down to it, not good for us" (Wallace 37). According to Wallace, watching TV [or in my mind, surfing the Internet as a social-network-aholic] can become malignantly addictive" (Wallace 38).

Although posters on social-networking sites are certainly self-conscious of their doings, they are not necessarily paralyzingly so. On the contrary, some would be the first ones to tell you that their very postings are freeing, liberating, that they allow them to be renewingly brand-spanking, all-new virtual people. They are able, via social-networking, to unleash themselves with pride into a brave new Internet world. To coin one of Wallace's phrases from his 1993 essay, "the 'unnatural' has become 'natural.'" Nowadays, we all seem to have an "unallergy to gazes" (Wallace 25). Indeed, people in today's Facebook-saturated culture have a veritable *addiction* to gazes.

This all leads ultimately, at least in *my* mind, to ponder what Wallace himself would have thought of social networking. Did he ever write about or respond in writing to it? I'm not sure whether he ever even *had* a Facebook or Twitter account. Nevertheless, in an interview he gave to Christopher Lydon on WBUR's *The Connection* program on February 21, 1996, two weeks after the release of *Infinite Jest*, Wallace displays an eerie prescience with regard to his own thoughts concerning the negative effects that the virtual remove of the Internet provides. In response to Lydon's assertion, in 1996, that "broadcast television is already dead and that the new world of interactive media, the Internet world, is an extension of that," Wallace responds,

> The fact of the matter is that it seems to me that if you still've got a nation of people sitting in front of screens, pretending, interacting

with images rather than each other, some needing more and more images, you're going to have the same basic problem, and the better the images get, the more tempting it's going to be to interact with images rather than people, and the emptier it's going to get.

It is true that social networking has the potential to further alienate people via the illusion of "connecting" them and bringing them together, for the patina, the crust of "togetherness" on any social-networking site, hides beneath its surface the reality that any "group" on Facebook or Twitter or like-minded communities consists of disparate individuals sitting *alone*, mentally if not physically, manipulating their keyboards and touchscreens and whatnot. As a culture, I do not believe we have reached, nor will we ever reach, a point at which a majority of people loathe the Internet. It has not yet lost its new-car aroma novelty. We are still too fascinated by it and its usefulness. Furthermore, I personally am not advocating anything remotely close to such a thing. Nevertheless, Wallace's concerns do, I believe, have ramifications with regard to the concept of *sincerity*.

Perhaps even more than television, the Internet and social-networking have led to what Wallace terms "a lost era of genuine conviction" (Wallace 54). I humbly ask you to ponder the question: How sincere *is* the average post on Facebook? What happens to sincerity when a majority of social-networkers eschew the real for the fabricated, the deliberately crafted? What *is* heartfelt expression, and what is performance? I certainly don't mean to overstate the issue. It's just that in my own experience of consuming and digesting many years' worth of social-networking content, sometimes I equate certain posts to making a "sincere" gesture of affection in a way that may be construed as more of a performance or spectacle rather than a *sincere* act of sincerity (asking for a significant other's hand in marriage over the loudspeakers during the seventh-inning stretch at Wrigley Field, for example) . I hope that no one in present company has personally *done* this. I definitely don't wish to offend….

In "E Unibus Pluram," Wallace argues that, as far as television is concerned,

> the most frightening prospect for the well-conditioned viewer, becomes leaving oneself open to others' ridicule by betraying passe expressions of value, emotion, or vulnerability…[T]he crime is naivete. Joe [Briefcase's] exhaustive…training in how to worry about how he might come across, seem to watching eyes, makes genuine human encounters even scarier, (Wallace 63)

as does, I would argue, the Internet and social-networking. It is much safer to protect oneself in a self-constructed carapace of irony, wherein, Wallace argues "[i]t [i.e. irony] has only emergency use. Carried over time, it is the voice of the trapped who have come to enjoy their cage" (Wallace 67). Furthermore, he states, irony, entertaining as it is, serves an almost exclusively negative function…[P]ersistent irony [is] tiresome. It is unmeaty…[O]ne ends up feeling not only empty but somehow…oppressed…[I]rony tyrannizes us…All U.S. irony is based on an implicit 'I don't really mean what I'm saying.' (Wallace 67)

It is hard to argue that in the present culture, sincere sincerity often can serve as an open invitation to be eaten alive, and the very nature of social-networking will always call into question the blurred line between genuineness and inauthenticity. Ultimately, intention is everything, and all one can do is make a conscious effort to travel roads, both real and virtual, making a deliberate attempt to be as *real* as possible.

Works Cited

Bennett, Shea. "This is How Much Time we Spend on Social Networks Every Day." *Social Times.* Prometheus Global Media LLC, 18 November 2014. Web. 25 May 2015.

Freedom, Joey. "[Rare] David Foster Wallace interview By: Chris Lydon Feb. 1996." Online video clip. *YouTube.* YouTube, 25 June 2014. Web. 11 April 2015.

Wallace, David Foster. *A Supposedly Fun Thing I'll Never Do Again.* New York: Back Bay Books, 1997. Print.

"My Slice of Sky": Irony, Belief, and the Shadow of DFW in Letham's *Chronic City*

David Laird

If a primary concern of postmodern (or post-postmodern) fiction is the nature of representation and the simulation of reality—along the lines of Jean Baudrillard's theory of simulacrum—then Jonathan Lethem's 2009 novel *Chronic City* is a key work to consider, especially as it relates to the influence of David Foster Wallace on contemporary U.S. fiction's move towards a heightened fascination with notions of transparency, spirituality, and post-secular belief. The imagined portrayal of Manhattan in Lethem's novel—and the navigation of the city by main characters Chase Insteadman and Perkus Tooth—establishes tension between the real-world city of New York as it is known through history, geography, and experience with an otherworldly version of the city. This bizarre version is replete with metaphorically laden features such as a gigantic, infrastructure-leveling tiger (22), a ubiquitous chocolate smell (173), and a massive land cavity purported to be a piece of art (108). Similarly, the novel's frequent references to authentic historical persons, including literary and pop culture personalities, is complicated by its uncanny inclusion of thinly-masked and alternatively-named allusions to a similar grouping of people and objects. The most prominent of these references in *Chronic City* is to the author Ralph Warden Meeker and his gargantuan novel *Obstinate Dust* (100)—a clear reference to David Foster Wallace and *Infinite Jest*—as there are a number of significant and lengthy descriptions and inclusions of the book.

Lethem's wedding of real persons with his fictional, hyperreal rendering of Manhattan operates under Brian McHale's notion of "transworld identities" (16-17)—which refers to a historical person's inclusion into a fictional world—and even takes this a step further in its insertion of the imagined (but analogous) references finding engagement with the characters throughout the novel, constituting a kind of simulacral transworld identity motif. This murky and complicated world of simulation is ultimately confronted by the only seemingly real and authentic image in Manhattan, a recurring 19th century Gothic church spire beyond the Dorffl Tower. The central protagonist, Chase Insteadman (a clever charactonym for simulated identity), frequently observes and reflects upon the spire, suggesting the possibility of hope and belief beyond the puzzling ontological labyrinth of the city. I offer that the significance of *Chronic City*'s heavy references to David Foster Wallace and *Infinite Jest*, in conjunction with the simulacral-versus-authentic dichotomy that the text sets up, links Lethem's literary ethos to Wallace's own positing of a post-ironic, post-secular reassertion of a notional belief in beauty, mystery, and transcendence in the face of the prevalent "incredulity towards metanarratives" (noted by Jean-Francois Lyotard) that characterizes postmodern literature.

Lethem's novel thus sets up a confrontation between the world of images and the possibility of an authentic site of belief through what critic Marshall Boswell would call an ironizing of irony (207), ultimately allying with Wallace's vision of fiction as a challenging force to the hopelessness of the postmodern worldview. This raises questions about what it means to deploy irony in order to affirm what Wallace calls "single-entendre principles" ("E Unibus Pluram" 81) and "passion, conviction, and engagement with deep moral issues" ("Joseph Frank's Dostoevsky" 271), rather than as a self-congratulating and clever trope of postmodernism. Further, *what* is signified by Lethem's invocation of the specific figure of Wallace in order to do so? I believe the answers to these questions are found in Wallace's unique place in literary history, as he wrote partially in reaction against the particular tendencies of postmodernism's castigation of spiritual belief, thus marking him as a key figure for Lethem to incorporate in his text.

In *Chronic City*'s progression from simulation to authenticity, the novel introduces a deluge of real-world popular culture and literary references, and, most notably, Ralph Warden Meeker's encyclopedic novel, *Obstinate Dust*, which evokes *Infinite Jest* through its matching syllable count, physical description, and the title's comedic play on the stubborn, immutable nature of addicted humanity. *Obstinate Dust*, Meeker's "opus" (103), like the text it signals, is "gigantic" (43), "raised above the others by the book's thickness," a "tome" (100), a "brick of pages" (101), a "big paperback" (102), and constitutes a "heft" that "must have been a thousand pages long" (100). Upon receiving the book from a friend, protagonist Chase Insteadman remarks, "I felt I'd incurred a responsibility, was somehow doomed to the book" (103), a sentiment that seems to reflect anxieties many people appear to have about reading *Infinite Jest*. Other references throughout *Chronic City* to *Infinite Jest*'s content, such as Laird Noteless' art installation entitled "Urban Fjord" (which is a city-block sized pit strewn with waste), allude to particular objects and themes in *Infinite Jest*, this one signaling the Great Concavity. A heavy reliance on marijuana, as "Chronic" in the title suggests (not unlike Ken Erdedy and Hal Incandenza's abuse in *Infinite Jest*), make references to Wallace's text patently recognizable. Similarly, a drug dealer named "Foster Watt" peddles marijuana to Perkus

Tooth in boxes made of Lucite (which incidentally is the same material that composes the walls quarantining the Great Concavity) (20). Additionally, similarly-syllabic titles akin to *Obstinate Dust* such as *Immaculate Rust* and *Adequate Lust* are remarked upon by the characters (374-5).

After reading only a brief portion of the giant novel, Insteadman pitches *Obstinate Dust* into the gaping Urban Fjord, saying: "*Obstinate Dust*, meet Obstinate Hole…it would be a relief to walk the return path without the asymmetrical sink-weight in my pocket. I gave the book a spirited heave, wrenching my shoulder in the process. The tubby paperback fluttered softly as it dwindled to a birdlike speck….Then it was gone" (111). In the final pages of the novel though, Insteadman acquires another copy of *Obstinate Dust*, an act of repentance for his earlier disdain for the book, feeling morally bound to read it in the wake of an adoring friend's death, saying "though it's hardly easy going, I'm doing my best to push through to the finish line, in Perkus' memory. I read it on the subway….Once in a while…I look up and see another rider with a copy of Meeker's bulky masterpiece in their hands, and we share a sly collegial smile, like fellow members of some terrorist cell," a clear nod to *Jest*'s dreaded wheelchair-bound Canadian A.F.R. insurgents (465). This expression of the unique solidarity of Wallace's readership (to which this conference is a testament), in conjunction with the moral gravitas ascribed to *Obstinate Dust*, serve as clues to *Chronic City*'s fascination with community and belief as they relate to contemporary literature. The great extent to which Lethem includes references to Wallace in his novel is thus significant, not just in terms of literary cachet, but, I offer, also in the sense of a perceived philosophical alignment with Wallace's ideals.

In contrast to the simulacral world that comprises Manhattan in *Chronic City*, one recurring landmark stands in opposition to the murkiness of the virtual, otherworldly state of unreality, offering the possibility of authenticity and a starting point for belief in something greater than the observable world: that of the church spire beyond the Dorffl Tower. Chase Insteadman engages with the spire on six occasions throughout the novel, most notably in the last scene of the book. His musings on the recurring spire's architecture and the avian life that abounds around it offer some hint at the possibility of an escape from, or at least a dissatisfaction with the vampiric, soul-sapping nature of the inauthentic Manhattan that ultimately claims Perkus Tooth as its victim and reveals Chase's life to be a farce. As in Hana Wirth-Nesher's discussion of urban space in modern fiction in her book *City Codes*, characters here engage with the mapping of "affect" within the "imaginative reconstruction of [their] own environment" (6), and this particularly applies to Chase Insteadman's engagement with the church tower as he manifests a kind of emotional and spiritual affect in his frequent consideration of the structure.

Chase's first sighting of the spire establishes a fascination or fixation on such affect, with the spire conveying a sense of curiosity: "I take a moment every day on waking to glance at it to see whether the birds are there" (67). The spire is first established in this passage as being "three or four blocks away, something built in the nineteenth century," with Chase having never sought out its name or exact location (67). Whatever the significance of the spire at this point in the text, Chase refers to it as "my slice of sky" (67), displaying an association of affective serenity, contemplation, and awe with the structure's orbit. The second description of the spire reveals greater significance, as Chase notes that "the church spire outside my window is the sole thing I look at deliberately, consciously, every single day" (124), evoking Walter Benjamin's notion of the authentic aura of artistic objects with Insteadman's affirmation of the spire's unique authenticity amidst an urban environment of simulation. The spire thus functions for Chase as a marker of reality amidst the unreality of Manhattan's simulacral existence, making it an important site of ontological value, as it marks the crisis between simulation and reality that the novel puts in tension. This dichotomy, in conjunction with the abounding references to Wallace, serve as a possible indication of the philosophical and literary positioning of Jonathan Lethem in Wallace's camp of unironic, empathetic fiction. At a late stage in the book, one character is described as having "eyes drowsy with congenital irony" and bearing "the promise of deadpan commiseration here" (30), a description that Wallace might readily apply to the present generation of those raised by television. Wallace's 1993 "E Unibus Pluram" essay—written around the time he began writing *Infinite Jest*—is about this very subject, that the hip, detached irony that characterizes the vast majority of televisual representation in the U.S. has radically influenced the landscape of contemporary fiction in America, to the point that the attitude of sardonic irony is a hereditary trait. Wallace eschews this kind of attitude, calling instead for what critic Lee Konstantinou characterizes as the generating of "forms of affect…via an ethos of postironic belief" (85).

In other words, the initial freedom of postmodernism's cavalier denial of spiritual authority ends up to be ultimately vacuous, and a desire for the reinstatement of belief is the existential fallout. For all *Chronic City*'s ironic wit and metafictional irony, Lethem gives the appearance of alignment with Wallace's stated views through his setting up of a simulacral universe that finds respite in the authentic site of the church spire, an edifice from which Chase Insteadman seeks solace from the world of simulation and which represents a practical site of faith and belief amidst a city of mere image. In this way, Lethem, like Wallace in *Infinite Jest*, uses irony to ironize the state of U.S. culture, offering instead a thoughtful and sincere approach to big questions about meaning, value, belief, and perhaps even theology and religion.

Chronic City ultimately poses a challenging universe where the virtual world becomes practically indistinguishable from the real one, wherein historical and real-but-obscured personages merge with the fictitious "mad island" of Manhattan (303). The most notable of these cryptic references finds an analogue in David Foster Wallace, whose *Infinite Jest* presents a similarly futuristic America rampant with techno-media, consumerism, waste, and addiction, not wholly unlike the New York that Lethem presents. Though Chase Insteadman never actually enters the church his spire is attached to, the eventual location of it in the book's final pages offers a possible clue to a hope in some kind of spiritually-based system that might render the world more objective, meaningful, and significant than the constructed simulacral one that causes such anxiety and confusion among the novel's characters. While it could be argued that the cathedral represents an antiquated and foreclosed old-world institution in the midst of Manhattan's new postmodern simulation, I offer that Chase's ground-level discovery of the church on the novel's final page, and his possessive identification that "Only after…did I judge the shape of the church's spire and knew that these were my birds, that we stood at the foot of my tower" (467) indicates an important moment of self-actualization and a meaningful personal connection to the place's authentic aura. While Insteadman's possessive claim on the church spire could be interpreted as a solipsistic moment of spiritual concavity, detached from wider expressions of faith as a communal experience, it nevertheless signals at least a burgeoning spiritual reflex in his character that seems to be largely absent among the other denizens of Manhattan throughout the novel.

In "E Unibus Pluram" Wallace envisions a category of American "literary 'rebels'" who "might well emerge as some weird bunch of anti-rebels, born oglers who dare somehow to back away from ironic watching…Who treat of plain old untrendy human troubles and emotions in U.S. life with reverence and conviction. Who eschew self-consciousness and hip fatigue" (81). Jonathan Lethem's portrayal of the spiritually curious protagonist Chase Insteadman may be the vehicle for one such form of rebellion, interrogating the network of simulation and image that marks millennial, televisual America, and opening the door, even just a crack, to the possibility of some alternative mode of ontology from that of the consumer utopia, "end of history" ethos which Wallace himself so urgently confronted.

Works Cited

Baudrillard, Jean. "The Precession of the Simulacra." *Media and Cultural Studies: Keyworks*. Ed. Meenakshi Gigi Durham and Douglas M. Kellner. 2nd ed. Malden: Wiley-Blackwell, 2012. 388-407. Print.

Benjamin, Walter. "The Work of Art in the Age of Mechanical Reproduction." *Media and Cultural Studies: Keyworks*. Ed. Meenakshi Gigi Durham and Douglas M. Kellner. 2nd ed. Malden: Wiley-Blackwell, 2012. 18-40. Print.

Boswell, Marshall. *Understanding David Foster Wallace*. Columbia: South Carolina UP, 2009. Print.

Konstantinou, Lee. "No Bull: David Foster Wallace and Postironic Belief." *The Legacy of David Foster Wallace*. Ed. Samuel Cohen and Lee Konstantinou. Iowa UP, 2012. 83-112. Print.

Lethem, Jonathan. *Chronic City*. New York: Vintage, 2009. Print.

Lyotard, Jean François. "The Postmodern Condition: A Report on Knowledge."

Modernism to Postmodernism: An Anthology. Ed. Lawrence Cahoone. Cambridge, MA: Blackwell, 1996. 481-513. Print.

McHale, Brian. *Postmodernist Fiction*. London: Methuen, 1987. Print.

Wallace, David Foster. "E Unibus Pluram: Television and U.S. Fiction." *A Supposedly Fun Thing I'll Never Do Again: Essays and Arguments*. New York: Back Bay Books, 1998. 21-82. Print.

---. "Joseph Frank's Dostoevsky." *Consider the Lobster*. New York: Little, Brown, 1999. 131-160. Print.

Wirth-Nesher, Hana. *City Codes: Reading the Modern Urban Novel*. Cambridge: Cambridge UP, 1996. Print.

A Restful Reverie
from "The Scissor Man"
Jeffrey Calzaloia

With a Whirl of Thought oppress'd,
I sink from Reverie to Rest.
—Jonathan Swift, "The Day of Judgment"

As I nodded off on the night of Sunday, September 7th, 2008—my thoughts loosening amid the chirping of crickets outside my bedroom's open window, the whispering of the wind, the rustling of the trees, the metronomish ticking of the cuckoo clock keeping time on the mantle[1]—and as my eyes lost equilibrium and subconsciously rolled up in their sockets, I barely registered sleep's soft embrace or dreaming that *I remember sitting in a stiff chair in a warm wood-paneled room in front of an older man with the look of an anthropomorphized turtle; and I asked if he had heard from his friend my father, if he'd considered the proposal we'd both outlined, and he said that yes he had spoken with my father and had heard the proposal and that he felt that I was indeed a promising candidate for the position in question, a tenured professorship in the English department he chairs at this college; and I responded by saying that not only was I a promising candidate but the perfect candidate by virtue of my polymathic tendencies, my exceptionally broad reading, and my truly scandalous memory, to which the man smiled and asked a question I hadn't anticipated; and I replied that no, I am not crazy, that what happened to me on that day has no effect whatsoever on the present, and then told him to name a poem, any poem, and that I could recite whatever poem he chose without pause; and the man considered this, stating a little-known poet's name and the title of one of said poet's even lesser-known poems, and off I went; and the man frowned when I finished my recitation and said that a good memory is nothing new, that they're a dime a dozen at most colleges already, at which point I was forced to up the ante*

1   I remember that I bought this particular horological beauty at an antique shop on Washington Street in Wellesley MA, an establishment presided over by an outwardly cordial but inwardly shrewd horsetrader who attempted to swindle me into paying far more for the clock (a passable copy of a Bavarian master's original) than it was really worth, a swindle I sidestepped by pointing out that his business wouldn't last long if Interpol was made aware of the black-market antiquities smuggling operation based out back, at which point he paid for my silence with the clock and told me to never darken his door ever again.

and remind him of the time Dad had helped him out of "a tight spot"; and the man put on a show of seeming sincerely unimpressed, but not before I saw his jaw's muscles slacken as the gulf between my statement and his response to it widened, and I was 97.84% certain that he would assent within the next ten seconds; and my observation proved accurate six seconds later when he reached down and opened one of his desk's drawers and lifted out and laid before me a sheaf of official-looking documents that he said I should fill out ASAP if I wanted to start here on September 8th, if only on a provisional basis before the dream of what happened on August 23rd, 2008 obliterated as the cuckoo clock sang its song and yanked me out of unconsciousness, the yank itself seeming heartless as I awoke and switched on the news—which, as the late Richard Jeni pointed out, should just be called "the bad news," because it's always been bad and probably always will be—the memory dissipating as I forced myself to blearily get out of bed and ready for my forthcoming first day as an instructor at Harper College.[2]

---

2   I remember that my initial run of research into Harper College re its suitability as a place of employment had veered off-course quite early on and become far more fixated on HC's founder and first president, the late Diane Morrison (which REMEMBER to q.v. §3, Memory 4, *supra*, for the biographical details), than on HC itself—possibly because I was scared (if only in a subconscious and therefore unaccountable way) of digging too deep into its hiring history and discovering that the odds of my actually getting the position were slim to none but probably because I'd already intuited (again, subconsciously) that the opposite was true, that I would indeed get the job and that that simple fact would then force me to make a commitment, or, as Rabelais, in a slightly different context, wrote, *S'asseoir entre deux selles le cul a terre.*

Himself's Figurants
Tom Winchester

Not contextualizing David Foster Wallace's *Infinite Jest* as within a specific style makes the novel seem like a sadistic joke. The only narratives which resolve are subordinate to the central one, and the impulse, after more than a thousand pages, is to start back at the beginning. The novel would seem unfinished, full of holes, and confusing without writers like Erich Auerbach, Hilton Kramer, and George Kubler who've laid the foundations for interpreting art and literature.

While reading *Infinite Jest*, there are several questions that beg to be answered. Reading it is almost like a treasure hunt of figuring out if Helen and Hugh Steeply are the same person, and if the Year of the Depend Adult Undergarment is actually 2009. Narratives like these serve as the novel's dominant climaxes even though they're peripheral to whether the *Samizdat* exists and where it's located. The master copy of the *Samizdat* is never found, and its existence is never confirmed, so, because of this, there is no climax to the novel's central narrative.

Instead, the pages of *Infinite Jest* focus on seemingly less important, every-day, banal things. The novel goes on endlessly about every minuscule detail of banalities like the tennis-warm-up schedule, the complete effects and compounds of complex drugs, and the actions of ancillary characters like Avril and Hal Incandenza, Don Gately, and Marathe. The novel's main character, James O. Incandenza, who is also referred to as Himself, only appears in the narrative as a child or a ghost despite the fact that if he were included as a living character we'd have a definite answer to both does the *Samizdat* exist, and where is it. He is the direct link between Enfield Tennis Academy and Ennet House, and he's the one who created the *Samizdat* and named it "Infinite Jest," but he's committed suicide before what the book considers the present day. As a result, the narrative is built by following less important characters doing less important things.

Such banality may seem pointless and annoying unless *Infinite Jest* is Wallace's attempt to convey a particular style. Erich Auerbach claimed in his book *Mimesis: The Representation of Reality in Western Literature* that style is determined by the way in which real life is represented, and he goes on to describe the history of styles from the days of Homer all the way until Virginia Woolf. In the case of *Infinite Jest*, real life is painted as a succession of seemingly unimportant moments, and it's because of this aspect that the novel is exemplary of the postmodern style.

Art critic Hilton Kramer wrote an essay in 1982 titled, "Postmodern Art and Culture in the 1980s," that makes a direct linkage between banality and realism. He does this with the inclusion of a quote from architectural critic Charles Jencks, who has written extensively on postmodernism. "It is realistic, because it accepts monotony, cliché and the habitual gestures of a mass-production society as the norm without trying to change them. It accepts stock response and ersatz without protest, not only because it enjoys both, finding them real, but because it seeks to find those usually disregarded moments of interest (the fantastic hidden in the banal)."[1]

This idea is anticipated by a passage from art historian George Kubler's 1962 book, *The Shape of Time: Remarks on the History of Things*. "Actuality is when the lighthouse is dark between flashes: it is the instant between the ticks of the watch: it is a void interval slipping forever through time: the rupture between past and future: the gap at the poles of the revolving magnetic field, infinitesimally small but ultimately real."[2]

Both Kramer and Kubler place emphasis on the banal, seemingly less important moments in life, and in combination with Auerbach's claim that style is determined by the representation of reality, Wallace's *Infinite Jest* seems to be perfectly fitting for what would be considered postmodern. It would be enough to support this idea in the text with allegorical examples like the fact that Orin Incandenza is anhedonic, Joelle envisions "The Ecstasy of St. Therese" by Gian Lorenzo Bernini, and Randy Lenz's main motivation is release, but the most illuminating example in this respect is a passage from late in the book when James O. Incandenza outlines his creative manifesto to Don Gately. The passage, which describes Incandenza's approach to filmmaking, including the concept of focusing on figurants instead of one central character, effectively serves as direct message from Wallace to the reader that provides the motivations behind the novel's style.

> The wraith says that he himself, the wraith, when animate, had dabbled in film entertainments, as in making them, cartridges, for Gately's info to either believe or not, and but in the entertainments the wraith himself made, he says he goddamn bloody well made sure that either the whole entertainment was silent or else if it wasn't silent that you could bloody well hear every single performer's voice, no matter how far out on the cinematographic or narrative periphery they were; and that it wasn't just the self-conscious overlapping dialogue of a po-

seur like Schwulst or Altman, i.e. it wasn't just the crafted imitation of aural chaos: it was real life's real egalitarian babble of figurantless crowds, of the animate world's real agora, the babble of crowds every member of which was the central and articulate protagonist of his own entertainment....Which is why, the wraith is continuing, the complete unfiguranted egalitarian aural realism was why party-line entertainment-critics always complained that the wraith's entertainments' public-area scenes were always incredibly dull and self-conscious and irritating, that they could never hear the really meaningful central narrative conversations for all the unfiltered babble of the peripheral crowd, which they assumed the babble(/babel) was some self-conscious viewer-hostile heavy-art directorial pose, instead of radical realism[3]

Infinite Jest conjures how it feels to never reach "The Show" nor "I.D.," especially when nearing the end of the novel and it becomes abundantly clear that the days, weeks, and months spent reading it really aren't going to produce the nice, all-loose-ends-tied-up kind of conclusion. The fact that the novel's central narrative doesn't resolve would seem like a setback if banality weren't a tenet of the postmodern style, but because of writings like those by Auerbach, Kramer, and Kubler, its representation of reality as a succession of banal events can be understood not as a joke, but a literary achievement.

[1] Hilton Kramer, "Postmodern Art and Culture in the 1980s" in *Revenge of the Philistines: Art and Culture, 1972-1984* (New York: The Free Press, 1985), 9.
[2] George Kubler, *The Shape of Time: Remarks on the History of Things* (New Haven: Yale University Press, 2008), 15.
[3] David Foster Wallace, *Infinite Jest* (New York: Back Bay Books, 2006), 835-836.

Modern American Lostness
(or how to be and not be alone)
Ashlie M. Kontos

> *A quarter of America is a dramatic, tense, violent country, exploding with contradictions, full of brutal, physiological vitality, and that is the America that I have really loved and love. But a good half of it is a country of boredom, emptiness, monotony, brainless production, and brainless consumption, and this is the American inferno.*
>
> —Italo Calvino

In choosing to research something "real American," what David Foster Wallace described as "something particularly sad…a stomach-level sadness… kind of lostness," I began researching, not Wallace's own texts, but those of his contemporaries and predecessors ("The Salon Interview" 59). Jonathan Franzen published How to Be Alone in 2002; just over ten years later, Jonathan Saftan Foer delivered a commencement speech entitled "How Not to be Alone." Frazen proposes that acts of substance, such as reading, are a remedy for loneliness: "Readers and writers are united in their need for solitude, in their pursuit of substance in a time of ever-increasing evanescence: in their reach inward, via print, for a way out of loneliness" (88). Conversely, Foer stresses fellowship. Individuals are now spending more time physically alone while being virtually connected, and though reading is still an option to generate emotional evolvement, Foer recognizes, "Technology celebrates connectedness, but encourages retreat. […] My daily use of technological communication has been shaping me into someone more likely to forget others[1]" (n. pag.). Throughout Wallace's fiction and non-fiction there resides

---

[1] In one of many conducted interviews, psychoanalyst Sherry Turkle recounts that eighteen year old Larry admits, "I don't apologize to people any more. I just put my excuses on as my status [referring to Facebook]. The people who are affected know who I mean" (233). Turkle goes on to conclude, "Technology makes it easy to blur the line between confession and apology, easy to lose sight of what an apology is, not only because online spaces offer themselves as 'cheap' alternatives to confronting other people but because we may come to the challenge of an apology already feeling disconnected from other people. In that state, *we forget that what we do affects others*" (*my emphasis* 234).

a ubiquitous tension between one's ability to be solitary and one's capacity to engage with others. Part of the tension delineated by these authors, admittedly, has to do with technology's overwhelming invasion into our private lives. In 1 996 at the onslaught of the telecommunications revolution, Wallace admitted, "[T]echnology is just gonna get better and better…it's gonna get easier and easier, and more and more convenient, and more and more pleasurable, to be alone with images on a screen" (Lipsky 86). Almost twenty years later, contact by screens is easier and often more prevalent than face-to-face communication[2], which makes us feel connected without actually being with one another. In exploring the therapeutic duality of solitude on the one hand and companionship on the other, I set out to investigate Wallace's insight into this modern American lostness: how we respond to discomfort, loneliness, and sadness and, more importantly, why we often respond in the unmindful ways that we do.

Before discussing how being solitary and/or being together relieves our American lostness, I would like to first recognize why it is so hard for many of us to even choose (re)engagement—either with the self or others. In short, why do we choose hours of television, the barrage of Facebook updates, Twitter tirades, etc. over engaged, present, untethered, intimate interaction? Answer: ease, convenience, pleasure—exactly the same reasons that Wallace delineated as to why people get sucked into watching screens in the first place. According to social critic Giles Slade, "[m]achines *can* dull the pangs of loneliness," but the more ominous reality is that such electronic/technological devices function to "distract us or to provide *prosthetic substitutes* for human company" (*my emphasis* 13). In the fast-paced, deadline oriented society we live and work in, virtual communication is now necessary, but it is only a succedaneum. Foer observes that communication technologies—texting, e-mail, voicemail, etc.—"were not created to be improvements upon face-to-face communication," instead they were created as "diminished substitutes" (n. pag.). Sadly enough, "[t]he problem with accepting—with preferring—diminished substitutes is that over time, we, too, become substitutes. People become used to saying little used to feeling little" (Foer n. pag.). People may use technology as a way to communicate easily with one another, but in the process we begin to treat one another differently. Psychoanalyst Sherry Turkle's data supports Foer's theory; she states: "Networked, we are together, but so lessened are our expectations of each other that we can feel utterly alone. And there is the risk that we come to see others as *objects to be accessed*—and only for the parts we find useful, comforting, or amusing" (*emphasis added* 154). People

---

2 According to a Pew study published in March 2012, "63% of all teens say they exchange text messages every day with people in their lives. This far surpasses the frequency with which they pick other forms of daily communication, including… face-to-face socializing outside of school (35%)" (n. pag.).

become objects that grant us pleasure when and how we prefer, and this happens partially because we access one another through devices. This is not technology's fault, per se; the way we use technology speaks more to our flaws, our inability to self-regulate. Though many scholars question the benefit-to-detriment ratio of technology in relation to our emotional capacities, science and business have fully embraced technology's blessings: convenience and speed; many have tried to reassure the public that technology will self-correct any complications that it creates[3]. Wallace was skeptical of the technology-as-boon theory. He admitted that, "The idea...that improved technology is going to solve the problems that the technology has caused seems to me to be a bit quixotic," and no matter how useful or progressive a device is:

> if you've still got a nation of people sitting in front of screens interacting with images rather than each other, feeling lonely and so needing more and more images, you're going to have the same basic problem. And the better the images get the more tempting it's going to be to interact with images rather than other people ("A Lost 1996" n. pag).

Just because something is easy/convenient does not mean it is fulfilling or even capable of providing us with the intimacy that we desire and need. Though face-to-face interactions require more time, energy, and effort, these complications lead to wholeness, a deeper connection that screen-images simply cannot fully provide. Yet we still seem to prefer ease. Wallace discusses the American culture's preference for technology, specifically television, in "E Unibus Pluram: Television and U.S. Fiction": "[T]he television screen affords access only one way...this is why television also appeals to such lonely people. [...] Lonely people tend, rather, to be lonely because they decline to bear the psychic costs of being around other human beings" (22). Turkle finds this conjecture to be quite true; she observes, "Today, our machine dream is to never be alone but *always in control*. This can't happen when one is face-to-face with a person. But it can be accomplished...by slipping through the portals of a digital life" (*my emphasis* 157). We trade intimate connections and communion for control and invulnerability. Brené Brown, now an internationally acclaimed

---

3   In her interview with Krista Tippet, Danah Boyd, principal researcher at Microsoft Research, discusses the initial hopes and dreams for the Internet in the early days of its inception. She recalls that many hoped the Internet, "would create a level of egalitarianism. It would be the freeing democratic mechanism for the world writ large. It would bring about the next Enlightenment, all of these big dreams. [. . .] And what intrigued me was that as these technologies became part of everyday life, what we saw is that people brought with them *all their flaws*" (*my emphasis* n. pag.).

4   Turkle also recognizes that, "Mobile technology has made each of us 'pauseable.' Our face-to-face conversations are routinely interrupted by incoming calls and text messages. [. . .] In the new etiquette, turning away from those in front of you to answer a mobile call or respond to a text has become close to the norm" (161).

researcher in social work, finds that, "[W]e've confused feeling with failing and emotions with liabilities" (35). As a means of self-preservation in an age of constant bombardment, technological or otherwise, we keep emotional engagements low and our walls high. We become less involved, less committed in tangible ways but more available via detached collaborations.

If it is difficult to be in communion with one another because of the "psychic costs" such interactions entail, it is just as challenging to be alone. In *Infinite Jest*, Hal ponders, "We are all dying to give ourselves away to something. . .the object seemed incidental to this will to give oneself away, utterly" (900). Wallace echoes his protagonist's concern in his interview with Lipsky; Wallace professes, "We absolutely have to give our power away" (88). We rarely, if ever, give our power to ourselves. We give it to others, to objects, to addictions, to forces and influences outside of our control. In giving our power away, we have less and less time/energy to be with ourselves in a healthy, reflective, nurturing state. In the overworked, always-on lifestyle many of us now lead, the ability to take time for ourselves is neglected. Turkle observes that, "Increasingly, people feel as though they must have a *reason* for taking time alone, a reason not to be available for calls" (*emphasis added* 202). As if well-being and personal nourishment are not reason enough. Christopher Long and James Averill explore the effects of solitude and conclude there are at least four benefits of solitude: freedom, creativity (this includes self-transformation and reconstruction of cognitive structures), intimacy, and spirituality[5]. But Long and Averill note that, "in order to benefit from solitude, the individual must be able to draw on inner resources to find meaning in a situation in which external supports are lacking" (40). Yet, we have become so accustomed to filling our intermittent time—sitting on the subway, riding an elevator, waiting at the airport terminal—with technological entertainment instead of using these moments for introspection, for observation, or for a moment of being "turned off" or "unplugged." Many seem to now lack the "inner resources" to turn idle moments—meaning the moments when no one is demanding your time and energy—into moments of reprieve, and Long and Averill conclude, "This perhaps explains why many people, when alone, engage in distracting rather than productive activities" (40). It is as if we do not remember how to power down, to be still, to sit with the discomfort of silence until it no longer seems uncomfortable but edifying. We fill up our time—even our free time—with activity (communication activity or otherwise), so we end up feeling like there is not enough time in the day to get everything done much less stay in close, direct contact with those we care about.

---

5   This does not necessarily mean religious spirituality. The authors know spirituality, "is also closely related to feeling of intimacy or connectedness to others and to the world. When in solitude…one can withdraw into the intimacy of spiritual encounter with oneself, one's environment, or one's God" (29).

And the anxiety of not having enough time in the day is nothing new. The modernists were greatly concerned about how regulated time affects the individual in an industrial society; the invention of the clock and wristwatch as devices that control human activities instead of the sun—this movement away from Nature—caused great concern in the early twentieth century. Since then, technology has proliferated, and it is now almost impossible to disengage oneself from it. We are always connected; technological communication allows us to be immediately available all of the time. If we are always connected and available, then we can always be productive; we can work from anywhere, anytime. The workplace continues to encroach on our private spaces. And so a culture of exhaustion[6] develops partly because we do not and sometimes cannot break ourselves away from the increasing demands of work, home, school, social pressures, etc. all of which are made more imminent by technology. In 2007, Wallace describes the prevailing American culture as one of "Total Noise" because of the "volume of info and spin and rhetoric and context that I know I'm not alone in finding too much to even absorb" ("Deciderization" 301). What he and others are describing is a constant, looming overstimulation. Turkle describes the negotiations we now go through because our constant and immediate availability: "Busy to the point of depletion, we make a new Faustian bargain. It goes something like this: if we are left alone when we make contact," by texting or using SNS, "we can handle being together" (Turkle 203). Spatial distance is now almost necessary for us to participate in daily relationships because we are inundated with communication 24/7. She goes on to conclude that, "We express ourselves in staccato texts, but we send out a lot…[s]o we get even more back–so many that the idea of communicating with anything but texts seems too exhausting. Shakespeare might have said, we are 'consumed with that which we are nourished by'" (207). That is the catch-22: we cannot tolerate being alone with ourselves so we use technology to keep us "connected," but because we are overwhelmed by the amount of communication demanded of us–at home, at work, at all hours of the day due to the inescapable company of our cell phones–the primary way that we remain connected is via our technological devices, via some physical remove from the demands of paying attention to the overwhelming amount of data and noise and presence of Real Life in the technological age. William Deresiewicz finds that contemporary friendships which are maintained primarily by technological communication are a "simulacra of my friends, little dehydrated packets of images and information, no more my friends than a set of baseballs cards is the New York Mets. […] Scanning my Facebook page gives me, precisely, a <u>'sense' of connec</u>tion. Not an actual connection, just a sense" (n. pag.). Turkle

6   See washingtonpost.com's "Exhaustion is not a status symbol" by Lillian Cunningham from Oct. 3, 2012.

agrees with Deresiewicz. She admits, "Alone (with our robots) we feel new connections. Together (with each other) we feel new kinds of isolation" (n. pag). New connections via technology requires consumption; these new kinds of isolation comes not only at the cost of our emotional aptitude, but also at the cost to our own pocketbook.

Admittedly, it is in companies' and corporations' best interest for us all to be "plugged in," to spend less time together and more time connected through technology, apps, and SNS. In *Made To Break: Technology and Obsolescence in America*, Slade details the infantile want within American technological markets: "In 2005 more than 1 00 million cell phone were discarded in the United States," and discarded does not mean recycled, "discarded cell phones represent a toxic time bomb waiting to enter America's landfills and water table" (2). This equates to 50,000 tons of functional but outdated waste; Wallace enthusiasts should have no hesitation in equating this Real Life dumping to the toxic trash repositioned to Canadian territories by the U.S. in *Infinite Jest*. Wallace comments on the extreme waste produced by Americans for the sake of our pleasure in his creative journalism as well as his fiction. Writing about his experience aboard the cruise ship Nadir, he discusses the quantity of nautical-grade fuel such a vessel requires: "It burns between 40 and 70 tons of this fuel a day"; for a week's vacation on such a ship, it will consume 280 to 490 tons of fuel (331). To be clear, I do not wish to suggest that much-needed vacations are bad, immoral, or always so harmful to the environment. What I would like to point out is that such events—or objects—of pleasure are often harmful in seen or unforeseen ways. In a consumer-driven economy, in which products become obsolete with each new season, the correlation between pleasure and destruction is strong. If we are not wanting, then we are not buying, yet the markets depend on their ability to churn out newer, "better" commodities and our insatiable hunger for more. Famed feminist bell hooks summarizes the United States' present emotional delinquency thusly: "While emotional needs are difficult, and often are impossible to satisfy, material desires are easier to fulfill" (106). This explains why there are large segments of the population who attend to their emotional needs via material-goods (i.e. TV, internet surfing[7], entertainment apps, shopping, the addiction-of-their-choosing) but who still feel a sense of emptiness because these things do not and cannot assuage our emotional needs. Wallace sought to understand the reasons why his generation and subsequent ones suffer such emotional depletion. In his 1 996 interview with Christopher Lydon,

---

7   Giles Slade notes that, "for every one of the 7 ½ hours most adolescents now spend online he or she spends ½ hour less with family members. Nonetheless it was in 2004 when [Michael] Bugeja first wrote: 'we visit home pages instead of homes but convince ourselves that we are interacting responsibly with family and friends simply because we are keeping up with their lives" (Turkle n. pag.).

Wallace admits, "Most of my friends are extremely bright, privileged, well-educated Americans who are sad on some level," and though he connects this sadness to loneliness, he believes the cause has something to do with what, "the culture has taught us (or [what] we've allowed the culture to teach us) that really the point of living is to get as much as you can and experience as much pleasure as you can and that the implicit promise is that will make you happy. I know that's almost offensively simplistic; the effects of it aren't simplistic at all" (n. pag.). Getting as much as you can, expecting the return of pleasure, and correlating pleasure to happiness creates a society permeated with comparison, dissatisfaction, and fear. Brown calls this a scarcity-culture. She finds that within such a culture, and according to her we are living in this kind of culture now, "Scarcity is the 'never enough' problem. [...] Scarcity thrives in a culture where everyone is hyperaware of *lack*. Everything from safety and love to money and resources feels *restricted*" and so individuals fixate on, "how much we have, want, and don't have, and how much everyone else has" (*my emphasis* 26). Wallace provides a prime example of this in "A Supposedly Fun Thing..." when the cruise ship Nadir passes by another bigger, newer cruise ship. He writes:

> I am suffering here from a delusion, and I know it's a delusion, this envy of another ship, and still it's painful. It's also representative of a psychological syndrome that I notice has gotten steadily worse as the Cruise wears on, a mental list of dissatisfactions and grievances that started picayune but has quickly become nearly despair grade... the dissatisfaction isn't the Nadir at all but rather plain old humanly conscious me, or, more precisely, that unAmerican part of me that craves and responds to pampering and passive pleasure: the Dissatisfied Infant part of me, the part that always and indiscriminately WANTS ("A Supposedly Fun Thing 315-16).

A culture that is overwhelmed with a sense of lack, which interacts on the basis of comparison, will always need more/want more in order to feel validated. The problem with this kind of lifestyle, especially regarding technology, is that it is intemperate; in seeking to fulfill some profound need for (self)worth via things or technologically-mediated relationships, we are always and will always be left wanting more. Wallace knew that this subject is not easy or pleasurable and even conceded that writing on it "was hard for me because it was about why exactly are we so sad and how have we become so unbelievably selfish, like lethally selfish and self-indulgent" ("A Lost 1996" n. pag.). The belief that having more and more would lead to happiness turns out to be a lie, but a lie that we have been living for far too long now. And Wallace warned the thing about lying is that, "it hurts to be lied to. It's ultimately that complicated: it hurts...it diminishes you, denies you respect for yourself, for the liar, for the world. Especially if the lies are chronic, systematic" ("Up Simba" 189). And this cultural lie is systematic; it is sewn by advertisers, the media, capitalists, politicians, our families, and by our fellow citizens. This is what we have been doing to each other generation after generation; we've been diminishing ourselves, albeit unintentionally or unbeknownst to us. Still, the dissatisfaction, unease, anxiety, and pain persists.

So this is what I have found from this research endeavor and what I propose: there is a strong correlation between discomfort and wholeness. Wholeness, equanimity, or well-being is not easily attained nor maintained. Though such a state of being may bring peace and joy, it is not earned without personal, committed effort. Wallace ponders the connection between strife and refuge in "Laughing With Kafka" (1999). He understands that, "[T]he horrific struggle to establish a human self results in a self whose humanity is inseparable from that horrific struggle. That our endless and impossible journey toward home is our home" (64-65). One's wholeness or humanity is not experienced without suffering; the two are bound up with one another, and it is this way perhaps so that in the movement towards wholeness of self we do not forget those around us, our community, and our fellow human beings who are also struggling to create their own self. Yet the overarching cultural message that we hear so much in the U.S. is that happiness is derived from things, from money, from getting what you want at the lowest cost or with the least amount of effort—passive pleasure. Three years before the Kafka piece, Wallace posed this question, "Is the real point of my life simply to undergo as little pain and as much pleasure as possible? My behavior sure seems to indicate that this is what I believe…But isn't this kind of a selfish way to live? Forget selfish—isn't it awful lonely?" (Wallace "Joseph Frank's Dostoevsky" 261). It would seem that our options are to either expend less effort interpersonally while investing more time in things that immediately gratify us—even though this kind of selfishness ultimately leads to loneliness—or we can take the risk of devoting ourselves to relationships and communities at the risk of being less solipsistic (perhaps even being disappointed at times) but with the potential payoff of those existential things that we ache for: love and belonging, emotional support, and human connection. But considering the scarcity-culture that we live in, Brown recognizes that transforming oneself is so challenging because, "there are enough of us struggling with the issue of worthiness that *it's shaping the culture*" (*emphasis added* 27). A culture that is struggling with its worthiness on an individual level produces the American lostness that Wallace so deftly cautioned as being a problem in 1990s and that has only continued to fester. Wallace's creative journalism, though so often "pants-wittingly-funny," is infused with serious, almost painful questions about us as citizens, artists, scholars, and as individuals (Crawford n. pag.). According to Kate Crawford,

Wallace found that journalism, despite its gravity, was a way of "filling up the tank of inspiration…to really sharpen and hone his fiction" (n. pag.). The discomfort of asking the hard questions through his journalist essays in turn inspired and strengthened Wallace's fiction. Anne Fadiman, a professor at Yale who lectures over Wallace's creative journalism, concludes her afterword in *The David Foster Wallace Reader* by recognizing that her students, "wish David Foster Wallace were alive, not only so he could continue to write but so they could ask him a question" (762). As Wallace fans and scholars who never had the chance to ask him questions directly, perhaps we wish he were alive, not only so he could continue to write but so that he could ask us questions about ourselves and inspire us in the pursuit of unflinching honesty. Yet, he did not leave us in the dark; he left us so many prisms of insight and encouragement: "[W]e are not dead but asleep, dreaming of ourselves" (*The Pale King*), so "Try to stay awake" ("Up Simba" 234), and "I wish you way more than luck" (This Is Water 137).

Works Cited

Boyd, Danah. "Online Reflections of Our Offline Lives." *OnBeing.com*. By By Krista Tippett. Minneapolis: MN, 2008. Web.

Brown, Brené. *Daring Greatly: How the Courage to Be Vulnerable Transforms the Way We Live, Love, Parent, and Lead*. New York, NY: Gotham Books, 2012. Print.

Crawford, Kate. "Remembering David Foster Wallace." Online video clip. *Big Ideas: The Smartest Stuff on TV Radio & Online*. ABC.net.au, 29 May 2009. Web. 16 May 2015.

Deresiewicz, William. "Faux Friendship." *The Chronicle of Higher Education: The Chronicle Review*. 6 Dec. 2009. Web. 19 Dec. 2014.

Fadiman, Anne. "Afterward." *The David Foster Wallace Reader*. New York: Little, Brown and Company, 2014. Print.

Foer, Jonathan Safran. "How To Not Be Alone." *The New York Times*. 2 June 2013. Web. 19 Mar. 2015.

Franzen, Jonathan. *How to Be Alone: Essays*. New York: Farrar, Straus and Giroux, 2002. Print.

hooks, bell. *All About Love: New Visions*. New York: William Morrow, 2000. Print.

Lenhart, Amanda. "Teens, Smartphones & Texting." *Pew Research Centers Internet American Life Project RSS*. 1 9 Mar. 2012. Web. 3 May 2015.

Lipsky, David, and David F. Wallace. *Although of Course You End Up Becoming Yourself: A Road Trip with David Foster Wallace*. New York: Broadway Books, 2010. Print.

Long, C.R., and J.R. Averill. "Solitude: An Exploration Of Benefits Of Being Alone." *Journal for The Theory Of Social Behaviour* 33.1 (2003): 21-44. Academic Search Complete. Web. 30 Apr. 2015.

Slade, Giles. *The Big Disconnect: The Story of Technology and Loneliness*. Amherst, N.Y: Prometheus Books, 2012. Print.

----. *Made to Break: Technology and Obsolescence in America*. Cambridge: Harvard UP, 2007. Print.

Smith, Aaron. "U. S. Smartphone Use in 2015." *Pew Research Centers Internet American Life Project RSS*. 1 April 2015. Web. 2 May 2015.

Turkle, Sherry. "Alone Together: Interviewing Sherry Turkle and Michael Bugeja." Interview by Giles Slade. *Huffington Post*. Huff Post Media, 2011. Web. 26 Mar. 2015.

----. *Alone Together: Why We Expect More from Technology and Less from Each Other*. New York: Basic Books, 2011. Print.

Wallace, David Foster. *The David Foster Wallace Reader*. New York: Little, Brown and Company, 2014. Print.

----. "Deciderization 2007–A Special Report." *Both flesh And Not: Essays*. New

York: Bay Back Books, 2012. 299-317. Print.

----. "E Unibus Pluram: Television and U.S. Fiction." *A Supposedly Fun Thing I'll Never Do Again: Essays and Arguments.* Boston: Little, Brown and Co, 1997. 21-82. Print.

----. *Infinite Jest: A Novel.* New York: Back Bay Books, 2006. Print.

----. "A Lost 1 996 Interview with David Foster Wallace." Interview by Christopher Lydon. *Arts, Ideas, and Politics with Christopher Lydon.* Radio Open Source, 2014. Web. 27 Mar. 2015.

----. *The Pale King: An Unfinished Novel.* New York: Little, Brown and Co., 2011. Print.

----. "The Salon Interview: David Foster Wallace." Interview by Laura Miller. *Conversations with David Foster Wallace. Jackson: University Press of Mississippi,* 20 1 2. 5 8-65. Print.

----. "A Supposedly Fun Thing I'll Never Do Again." *A Supposedly Fun Thing I'll Never Do Again: Essays and Arguments.* Boston: Little, Brown and Co, 1997. 256-353. Print.

----. *This Is Water: Some Thoughts, Delivered on a Significant Occasion, about Living a Compassionate Life.* New York: Little, Brown, and Company, 2009. Print.

----. "Up, Simba: Seven Says on the Trail of an Anticandidate." *Consider the Lobster And Other Essays.* New York: Bay Back Books, 2006. 1 56-234. Print.

Dreams Are Slaughtered Here Too

Rich Hanson

"Dreams Are Slaughtered Here Too" is a short story that explores somewhat the same theme that David Foster Wallace addresses in his essay "Consider the Lobster," a rumination that delves into the moral conundrum of boiling a creature alive in order to enjoy consuming it. The young man whose poem is the centerpiece of the story that I'm about to read is rebelling against the workplace that necessity has driven him to. He's aghast at the brutality and monotony of labor in a slaughter house and questions what it does to one's soul.

David Foster Wallace, at one point in his essay compares the brutality of slaughter to the carnival atmosphere of the lobster bake that he attended when he says …"Try to imagine a Nebraska Beef Festival at which part of the festivities is watching trucks pull up and the live cattle get driven down the ramp and slaughtered right there on the World's Largest Killing Floor or something—there's no way."

We pass the cattle and the hog trucks on the highway every day, giving little thought to the destination and fate of the creatures that are being hauled to slaughter. This refusal to dwell on such things, this compartmentalization of our role in the food chain, allows most of us to savor the role of a carnivore, relishing the flavor of a burger or a steak without suffering pangs of guilt. Sensitive people, those with empathy toward all living things do though, as did David Foster Wallace.

"The most important point here, though," Wallace states in another portion of the lobster essay, "is that the whole animal cruelty and eating issue is not just complex, it's also uncomfortable."

Dreams Are Slaughtered Here Too

The fifteen minute morning break was almost over. I looked at the drawing of a horse's head that I'd sketched on a notepad. It was pretty good. I'd captured the flaring of the nostrils, and the stallion's eyes radiated a defiant, untamed look. Not bad. Of course, I'd always been good at art. A guy has to make a living pursuing something other than dreams though, so I ended up here, a foreman in a meat-packing plant. My artwork now is pretty much confined to doodling. Throwaway art. A guy's got to have money in order to pursue an art career....money and/or influential backers. I couldn't come up with either one.

A knock at my office door summoned me back to business. I slid a slaughter report on top of my sketch just before the door opened. It was Mickey Kincaide, a slender, blond-haired young man whom I'd watched grow up a couple doors down from me. He was holding his knives, scabbard, mesh gloves, and apron.

"I just stopped in to thank you for giving me the chance to work here," he apologized, his head down to avoid looking at me. "But I just don't think I can handle it anymore."

I looked at him, surprised. He was a damn good worker as far as I was concerned. A good kid, too. A typical case of a nice kid whose hormones had gotten him into trouble. His parents were from the rigid "Old School" morality.

You know, "You screw up and now you've got to make it right." Now the kid is married to his 17-year old girlfriend and they have a young daughter to take care of. "What are you going to do, Mickey?" I asked him.

"I don't know," he replied dejectedly. "I'll find something else, I guess."

"You know," I reminded him, "in this depressed economy, this plant is one of the best paychecks in town."

"I know," he admitted, hanging his head a bit more. He pulled around a chair with his foot and set his equipment on it. Then he dug into his pocket and pulled out a piece of paper.

"I showed this to my old man," he said. "He called me 'a damn fool' and told me to get my head on straight. He said 'God damn it kid, you've got responsibilities now. Buck up and be a man.'"

I looked at the paper in astonishment. "You wrote a goddamned poem about quitting your job?" I asked him.

He nodded, then whispered, "Yeah."

I stared at him, catching a hesitant note in his voice. It sounded like he wanted to say more, but was gauging whether I'd be receptive or not. Finally he blurted out, "I showed it to Sarah, and she understood."

"Your wife," I reminded him sharply, "is a 17-1/2-year-old girl who reads romance novels and still feels bad about missing her senior prom. My God, Mickey, you were an A student. You had a helluva future ahead of you. If the two of you were so hell-bent on screwing around, why the devil didn't you have enough sense to at least take some precautions?"

He hung his head but handed me the paper. "I brought this because I figured it might make you understand why I'm leaving. I watched you as I grew up," he reminded me. "I know that you went to college and majored in art. Here," he insisted. "Read it."

THE SLAUGHTER PLANT by Mickey Kincaide

Terrified, the dumb brutes panic at being driven
They smell and sense the death that lurks beyond the doorway.
Their only escape from the electric shock prod though,
Is that ominous exit. A madness born of the fear of pain
Drives the beasts into the mechanics of slaughter.

The thunderclap of a rifle shot rocks its bovine brain.
The animal drops. Its hind legs are then tightly shackled
And its body yanked ceiling-ward so the throat-slitter
Can pierce its jugular vein with barbarian finesse,
His rubber boots sloshing through a morass of blood.

At times the animal reaches the throat-slitter
Still weakly kicking, still clutching at existence
Through a panic of uncomprehending pain.
Its doom has been pre-ordained though as it meets
The remorseless attack of the God with a knife.

Two hundred and eight-five head of beef an hour
Will be processed with calculated precision.
That's the brutal, inexorable certainty
Beneath the din and the frenzied activity,
The callous constant movement of the chain of death.

The headers, bung-droppers, belly-openers, gut-snatchers,
Kidney-poppers, split saw operators, shavers, lard pullers,
Hock cutters, skinners, hide pullers, bone-grinders,luggers,
The blood-dryers, the cookers, the gang in offal pack,
All move in like jackals to devour the corpse.

They all participate in the rendering of life
Into lard, table cuts, boneless trim, fertilizer,
Gelatin and hides. All are hardened to the horror,
Helmeted like the SS Guards who took a smug pride
In their processing of so many "sub-humans" an hour.

"Good God!" I growled, half astonished and half-angry that he could portray my livelihood in such a manner. "Is that all you see these guys I work with as, a bunch of goddamned Nazis?"

"Don't misunderstand me," Mickey protested. "It's not the people that work here that bother me. It's what they've become. Am I the only one here who sees the horror in what we are doing? The mind-numbing despair of a man who has to snatch the guts out of each carcass that moves past him and toss them into a pan. What kind of life is that? Or worse, what does Jenny Hodges think of day after day as she stabs the jugular vein of each neck that moves past her and watches the blood gush from it? Have the rest of you become so hardened? Don't you see that dreams are being slaughtered here, too?"

"It's not a matter of being callous, or hard," I explained. I had to pause and grope for the right words. What I finally came up with though, sounded rather banal.

"It's just doing what has to be done."

Mickey gazed at me with a look that mingled disappointment and contempt. I was failing to get through to him. Somehow I had to convince him that his feelings were something to be overcome. They were almost "unmanly."

"You know, Mickey, in all your experience with them, have you ever had a kid tell you 'I want to work in a packing house when I grow up?'"

"I didn't realize there was such a thing when I was a kid," Mickey admitted. "I guess I just thought that steaks were always steaks."

"I didn't know anything about packing houses either," I reassured him. "But there came a time in my life when I had to knuckle down and get a job to support myself and my family. A guy with a family learns to do what has to be done in order to survive. Even if you don't like it at first."

Mickey shrugged. "Why don't you read the rest of it?" he suggested. I could tell that he was uncomfortable with being preached to. He had probably heard similar raised-voice rhetoric from his father. Why should he stand here and take it from me? I did as he suggested and began to read from where I had left off.

Their scabbards clanging against their bloody chain belts,
The helmeted Kill-floor crew files out for lunch,
Removing their mesh gloves, their wrist guards, their ear plugs
And their aprons before they wash the blood from their hands.
Fragments of their conversation reverberate through the cafeteria.

They talk of sports...
"Think the Bucks have a chance against the Bulls tonight?"
They talk of women...
"I met this gorgeous bitch last night at Callahan's... man..."
They talk of money...
"I put 18 hours of overtime in so far this week."

Apparitions of the men who pulled the gold teeth,
Led victims to the showers, stoked the ovens, took head count
Of the trainloads of frightened humanity being herded into camp;
They gaze upon the lunchroom scene and knowingly smile
With an understanding rooted in their death-camp kinship.

It was thus at Auschwitz, Ravensbruck and Dachau.
Carloads of human cattle were ruthlessly dispatched
With businesslike Aryan efficiency, as blithely
As we kill now to placate a growling stomach.

So it will be in the next war to come as well.
The mechanics of slaughter that we serve, win or lose,
Will be paid for in souls that have atrophied;
That have shriveled into a hardness that feels no pity,
That grants no mercy; that no longer knows
Or cares anymore about examining their actions;
Men that have forgotten how to love or forgive.

I don't wish to become a man like that.

I handed the paper back to Mickey who took it from me without comment.

"You've got a gift for language, kid. You probably don't belong here," I told him, putting my hand on his shoulder as a gesture of friendship.
More or less, I was trying to tell him that I didn't take offense at what he wrote and that I appreciated his honesty. I wanted to leave the door open, in case he would reconsider and decide to stay on.

"I've seen your sketches," he said, lifting up the slaughter report to show me my notepad beneath it. "You don't belong here either."

"It pays the bills. What will you do to live?" I asked him.

"I'll give McDonalds a try. Maybe Pizza Hut," he said hopefully. "I'm young enough to work my way up to be a manager someday."

"You could do the same thing here," I reminded him.

"No, I can't," Mickey said. "I just don't think that I belong here." He made a move toward the door as if he were a feral cat accidently trapped in someone's garage. Every nuance of his demeanor seemed focused on "escape."

"You'll be back," I said sternly. "You'll get tired of flipping burgers for $8.50 an hour when you can make twice that much here."

Mickey turned toward me again, one hand still on the door handle and said, "I won't be back. There's got to be more to life than this!"

His total rejection of my livelihood and the friendly advice that I'd tried to give him finally got under my skin. I lost my temper. "Why!" I yelled angrily. "Because you demand that there should be? You haven't even begun to be disappointed, kid. You're just a kernel of corn that the millstone of life is beginning to grind on. When your old lady is bitching because she has no money to buy your daughter's formula, or when she turns her back on you in bed at night because you didn't bring home enough money to buy her that pair of new Reeboks she wants, then you'll be back! And damned glad to be back!"

"I don't think so," Mickey said coldly, as he turned his back to me, pulled the door open and slipped out of the office into the hallway.

Silently I wished him luck. He would need it.

My notepad with the head of the proud, untamed stallion, his nostrils flaring, his indignation at my attempt to capture him in a sketch lay on my desk still. Yeah, I maybe could have been a pretty decent artist, given a few breaks, but...what the hell. Who said life was fair?

I reached down, ripped the page from the notepad and crumpled it into a neat little ball. From my desk it was just a short bank shot off the cement brick wall into the wastepaper basket in the corner. Two points. It was time to go back to work.

I'm So Totally Identifying It's Not Even *Funny*

Danielle S. Ely

The first time I read it was in 2009 in a three-week summer graduate course. The second time I read it was the following semester for a "Complexity in Contemporary Narrative" course, and the third time I read it was in preparation for my Master's Thesis which I finished in 2011 (to make sure I got things right). Interestingly, the third reading was probably the most relaxed, i.e. the one closest to "reading for fun," but still, I have never read *Infinite Jest* outside the world of academia. Though that may be true, let the record show that I never resisted. Not one bit. And I had fun every single time I picked it up.[1]

First Reading: Summer 2009 was only my second semester as a graduate student. I had moved out of my parents' home to a small studio apartment in the student ghetto of Albany, NY to start grad school just that January. I was single, nearing asexuality, already fed up with the promiscuous party lifestyle everyone in Albany already had or seemed to want. I was unemployed and a bit embarrassed to have made it out of my parents' home only to have them pay for my apartment. Without air conditioning in that small studio apartment, I can remember lying horizontally on the floor in just my underwear, suffering my first real bout of depression, wondering if I had the gumption to make it through grad school. A few days later, I got *Infinite Jest* in the mail.

Earlier that summer, Dr. Kim Middleton, professor of ENG 590: *Infinite Jest*, kindly warned us that for this course, a.k.a this novel, we were going to need multiple bookmarks and that we should have the first eighty-seven pages read before the first night of class. The course would begin on August 3, at 6pm. We'd meet three days a week for three weeks ending August 16. And that's what intimidated me: the course, not the novel. Even after I took the novel out of the mailing slip and saw how dauntingly large it was, I still wasn't afraid of it. After all, I've never been afraid of a novel. I've never failed at reading. Sure, I've given up on some and claimed to have read when I hadn't, but this wasn't my first rodeo. I had once read nine William Faulkner novels in sixteen weeks in undergrad, so wasn't I ready for a long difficult novel even at such a quick pace?

What I didn't feel prepared for was the fact that our first night of class was not going to be the typical "first night of class." We weren't going over the syllabus and then getting out early. *Infinite Jest* was our syllabus, and if we got through the first eighty-seven pages on our own, we would have a pretty clear idea about what we would be in store for in the next three weeks.

So I read the first eighty-seven pages of *Infinite Jest* just like I had every other novel I had ever read; intimidating or not, complicated or not, I read. I found it delightful, a bit confusing, but I was eager to read on. I let the characters, themes, and storylines wash over me and then at 5pm on August 3rd, I walked the three blocks to class, down Albany's notoriously uneven sidewalks, in wedges, avoiding shattered glass along the way, hoping there might be a cute boy in my class to impress.

And of course there was a cute boy in my class that night, leaving me, an already socially anxious person, shy and quiet. And maybe that was why I remember being at a loss for words. But then again, Hal and the E.T.A. narrative are the first things we're introduced to in *Infinite Jest*, and traditionally, those characters and narratives usually turn out to be pretty important, so why not? Middleton had warned us all to be on the lookout for handholds, and so I was relieved to find that the rest of my classmates almost naturally divided their attention, reaching for the broadest, most easily accessible narratives to get through the sea of characters, themes, plots, and symbols. The professor and I, for the most part, stayed on Hal and the E.T.A. narrative, two other students followed the Marathe and Steeply sections, and the three remaining students explored the Ennet House/AA narrative. Waldman writes, "Saint Rose professor Kim Middleton led her class through the book in a discussion that started with suicide, then roamed to attitudes toward tennis, tattoos and the landscape of Boston. There was also talk of crack smoking and doomed love stories. And that was just in reference to the 100 pages they had read in the last 24 hours." As the first night of class ended, I remember deciding to take meticulous notes on the novel from then on…not because the difficulty of the novel made me feel I needed to, but mostly to save face in front of the five other graduate students who seemed to have a lot more to say about the novel than I did. The irony is that my classmates would end up making fun of my journal full of notes, calling me an overachiever. They'd laugh at my copy of *Infinite Jest* that today looks like it spent some time with Eraserhead on vacation. But the joke's on them, because look who's left talking about it. Or maybe the joke's on me, because they got out.

After class, I felt reinvigorated. From then on I was going to read *Infinite Jest*, take my notes, and say smart things about it in class. After all, I didn't have much else to do (remember I was unemployed and single). This was just what you did in grad school. But just one block away from campus, on the return walk to my studio apartment, I sprained my ankle. The wedges, which would obviously win me a potential mate, no longer seemed like an educated decision. If I wasn't already a young student trying to find a path through school; if I wasn't depressed, prone to lying horizontally on the floor, prone to being quiet on the verge of silent, approaching asexuality, then spraining my ankle after that first day of class really sealed the deal when it came to my identification with Hal. I found parts of myself in Hal. I found parts of myself elsewhere in the text too. Most importantly, though, I was beginning to find myself in grad school.

Reading *Infinite Jest* in an academic setting brings with it the benefit of reading in/with a built in 'community.' Though our actual 'community' was small with only six students and one professor, Middleton smartly designed the course to address broader concerns. On the about page for ENG 590, she writes:

> In this intensive summer course, our first and primary goal will be to read and discuss the entirety of Wallace's master work, *Infinite Jest*. In addition, however, we'll take stock of the critical responses to the novel, both professional and participatory. In the end, we'll hopefully arrive at preliminary answers to three fundamental questions: 1) Which kinds of interpretive approaches/habits does the novel encourage in its readers? 2) What does this novel reveal about the landscape of contemporary literature? 3) Given the current cachet of the novel and its author among a variety of audiences, what, if anything, can those trained in English Studies contribute to the conversation, and what skills would they need to do so?

Middleton's framework for the course was not only a fitting exploration of *Infinite Jest*, but coincidently a fitting explication of the existential crisis I was in at the time. I often speculated: Do I even have what it takes to be an English scholar? To be sure I wondered, "What, if anything" could *I* "contribute to conversation?" And on top of all that, Middleton now expected me to do these things in response to a book that was clearly smarter than me.

Fortunately, the small community of English scholars I belonged to wasn't my only lifeline. When Middleton announced that there was a Wallace listserv, I immediately created a separate gmail account (as she warned the inbox would be flooded by 10-20 emails per day) and have been reading and participating in the email threads ever since. Not only that, but *Infinite Summer* had launched just weeks before. On August 11th we "pulled even with the *Infinite Summer* group" (Middleton). Though we quickly outpaced the *Infinite Summer* reading schedule, the discussion threads and alternate 'community' of readers both that and the listserv provided, proved to be invaluable resources to six graduate students embarking on Wallace's work for the first time.

Scott Waldman, a writer for Albany's *Times Union*, was so impressed with our "staggering pace of 100 pages per day," he interviewed our class after we had "just finished the first of a three-week slog through the book," for his piece called "Surely You 'Jest.'" In it, he called us "brave," as if we must have been crazy to sign up for this. But I saw myself and my classmates as neither "brave" nor crazy. Though we brought to the table sophisticated reading strategies developed through years of schooling and experience, *Infinite Jest* is a book where no one gets the upper hand when it comes to "getting it." What I mean by that is: my status as a scholar doesn't make my reading/interpretation of *Infinite Jest* any better than anyone else's. I might look for different things, and even see different things in *Infinite Jest* than someone reading it outside of academia, or someone reading it "just for fun," but not because I have a better idea about how it operates. I'd say the only advantages that reading *Infinite Jest* as a scholar gives me are access to the right vocabulary, lenses, and theories through which I am able to articulate responses I have to the text, whether I read it in an academic setting or not.

In quoting Matthew Baldwin, Scott Waldman writes, "The Saint Rose students may be in one of only two college-level classes nationwide reading the book right now…but they certainly have a lot of company." On August 11, on the ENG 590 home page, Middleton wrote a post called "Infinite Summer et Toi." She writes, "Just a quick heads up: we've been very generously given a brief shout-out from the good people at infinite summer…No pressure or anything. Just say smart things. :)" It is moments like that that made me realize that these two seemingly separate communities—one comprised of scholars, the other of enthusiasts—were watching each other, were reading and considering each other's arguments; that we were really a part of one big community: a community of people who have read *Infinite Jest*…who finished…who read the footnotes and everything. Both communities enriched the reading experience of the other.

And then of course there's the whole matter of the fact that I read *Infinite Jest* again in the fall, the very next semester, with the very same professor, for her "Complexity in Contemporary Narrative" course. Of course, to some of my classmates, reading *Infinite Jest* again, or even for the first time, was a 'task' considering the number of other works we were going to cover and the fact that we were reading *Infinite Jest* at the tail end of the semester. More than a few admittedly skipped the footnotes. I didn't, but I did find the experience more relaxed. Instead of keeping track of what happens to whom (thanks to my notes from the previous semester) I was able to focus more on themes and characters I had ignored while clinging to my initial handholds.

At the time, I was also enrolled in "Intro to Literary Theory." As soon as we began reading and discussing feminist theory I felt a huge shift in the way I engaged with *Infinite Jest*. Initially, feminist theory made me feel like I had betrayed my gender by prioritizing Hal and the E.T.A narrative over poor Joelle, Avril, Kate, and Wardine. Wasn't I a big joke in the E.T.A. T-shirt I had made with "Hal Incandenza" printed on the back? But eventually I realized that I wasn't a joke and I hadn't betrayed anyone. On the contrary, feminist theory, especially feminist reader-response theory, gave me the tools and language required to articulate the shift in my priorities from one reading to the next. It allowed me to explore a feminist reading of *Infinite Jest*, which ended up becoming my seventy-page Master's Thesis.

In due course, feminist theory allows "new knowledge" to be possible, and to a novel like *Infinite Jest*, this notion is hugely important. Instead of using traditional interpretive modes that try to pin *Infinite Jest* down, like I tried to do when I read it the first time, feminist theory and the "elegant complexity" of *Infinite Jest* showed me that texts can actually be and mean more than their surface appearances. It is this discovery that answers Dr. Middleton's "preliminary" questions: the idea that my unique skills and experience encourages non-traditional readings of *Infinite Jest* and the fact that non-traditional readings complement the genius of *Infinite Jest* so well, marks the real value of my contribution to the conversation as an English scholar.

(Endnote)
1   The point is, I've never read *Infinite Jest* outside the realm of academia—never "just for fun." But however academic my reasons for reading the novel may have been, the side effects were clearly enjoyable enough to keep me talking about it six years later and to bring me to conferences around the country from New York to California and Illinois. In fact, I enjoy talking about this novel so much; I travelled all the way to Madrid, Spain, just to give a ten-minute presentation.

I have been able to talk about *Infinite Jest* in non-academic settings. Reading *Infinite Jest* in that summer graduate course was a topic of conversation partially responsible for initiating the six-year relationship I've had with my partner and "co-ponderer" Tony, who has travelled with me to every conference, and the archives in Austin, and who is of course in the audience today. He too has read *Infinite Jest*, only to some extent from my bidding. Unlike me, he had the pleasure of reading *Infinite Jest* outside of academia, at his own pace, though there may have been some pressure from me to finish quickly so that we would have even more to talk about.

The Pharmacology of *Infinite Jest* (or the deal with the missing DMZ)

Eric Izant

Hal's story in *Infinite Jest* begins with a memory of eating mold. As a young child he presents his mother with a handful of multi-colored mold scooped from the basement wall and proudly announces: "I ate this." It's suggested that Hal's early ingestion of mold is the symbolic cause of his inner losses, for despite becoming on the outside a successful athlete and gifted prodigy with an eidetic memory, Hal feels completely empty on the inside, devoid of any real self. By the end of the novel, Hal is able to discover his inner voice, but at the cost of his ability to communicate with the outside world. This transformation is sparked by a mysterious substance whose identity is unclear.

There are a number of theories regarding the source of Hal's change, but they all involve some sort of drug. Hal's transformation is shown to begin most acutely in the days after he quits smoking marijuana, his previous "substance of choice." This causes Hal to enter a state of withdrawal and leaves him feeling a sort of existential purposelessness. He wakes up one morning from a nightmare about a zoo and realizes his state of inner captivity: "It occurred to me that without some one-hitters to be able to look forward to smoking alone in the tunnel I was waking up every day feeling as though there was nothing in the day to anticipate or lend anything any meaning" (853). Hal's acknowledgment of his inner emptiness and chemical dependency creates the psychic space necessary for him to undergo a radical shift in perspective, a necessary step if he is to transition from the waste and sterility of addiction to the possibility of a new, sober life. However, he needs something else to complete this transformation: a drug called DMZ.

The presence of DMZ looms like a specter throughout the text, but what is most remarkable is that we never actually see it being taken. Although Hal and his friends, Pemulis and Axford, spend the majority of the book making plans for a big DMZ trip, the anticipated moment never occurs. The DMZ goes missing first, its hiding place empty, ransacked by an unknown entity. This happens on the same morning as Hal's nightmare, suggesting either that Hal took the DMZ himself or was drugged by somebody else. So, there are two questions for us to consider. First, what happens to the missing DMZ in the context of the narrative itself? And second, what, if anything, does Wallace mean by performing this storytelling sleight-of-hand?

To answer these, we'll start by examining what the novel can tells us about DMZ. So just what is DMZ? Well, in the text it's described as a hybrid mixture of a lysergic and a muscimoloid; these terms refer to the ergot fungi from which LSD is synthesized and an alkaloid found in mushrooms, particularly the magic variety. DMZ clearly then belongs to the psychedelic class of drugs, and all of these drugs happen to be produced from various types of mold. As it turns out, DMZ is also a psychedelic and a mold; in fact, it's a mold that grows on another mold, and possibly derived from the same mold that Hal ate as a child. Understanding DMZ as a psychedelic mold will help us interpret its role in Hal's transformation.

Let's begin our investigation by looking at the scene in which Hal likely ingests the DMZ to see if we can figure out how it gets into his system. The morning of his nightmare about the zoo, Hal wakes up in the panic of withdrawal. He goes to the bathroom to brush his teeth, then proceeds into the hallway where he encounters his classmate Ortho Stice. They talk about paranormal events—Stice has been haunted by a ghost, most likely the ghost of James, Hal's dead father—and Hal also mentions the recent school-wide drugging of unattended toothbrushes by an unknown perpetrator. This seemingly random fact makes sense if we consider the possibility that Hal has also just been drugged via his toothbrush, perhaps by his father's ghost, because it's not long after he brushes his teeth that Hal's reality starts to become increasingly distorted. Despite the literal improbability of a ghost drugging a toothbrush, this scenario feels more likely than the possibility that Hal takes the DMZ on his own. It's established that the ghost can physically affect objects; Pemulis later discovers his stash of DMZ has been ransacked, the ceiling tiles it was hidden above have been smashed to the floor. Although Hal is usually quite vigilant about keeping his toothbrush in sight, he has a few notable lapses of attention in this scene. For example, earlier in the bathroom, right before he brushes his teeth, Hal sticks his head out an unexpectedly open window to watch a winter storm. Is it possible that James's ghost drugs Hal's toothbrush while his back is turned? Whether or not it actually happens, the scene is a potent image of infection, of intrusion, with the chaos of the storm creeping into the safe world of E.T.A. as Hal unsuspectingly sticks his toothbrush into his mouth.

This symbol, the contamination of within from without, is predominant in the novel. We have it in the story of the mold Hal eats as a child, and in the constant reference to mouths, teeth, and toothbrushes. Let us not forget Gately's own nightmares about teeth and his own prank of contaminating toothbrushes, which the less said about the better. On a broader level, drug use by all the various addicts in the novel is another form of infection, the enslaving of the inner self by a poisonous foreign substance. There is something rotten in the heart of Enfield Tennis Academy. At one point a gang of younger students are exploring the dark ventilation tunnels under the school and find a fridge rampant with smelly mold. So when, after brushing his teeth and finding Ortho Stice Hal proceeds to set his toothbrush down on a vent and again turn his back, I can't help but imagine some kind of sinister mold spores being sucked through the air shafts from the dark, rotten cavities below the school and infecting the sterile hallways, Hal's toothbrush and eventually his mouth, stomach, and soul–their ultimate destination. It's telling that this corruption seeps out of the same tunnels where Hal goes to get high in secret, the very source of his spiritual rot.

With all of these references to Hal becoming infected, it's worth wondering why James would seemingly poison his own son with an incredibly potent drug like DMZ. To answer this, we need to look a bit more at the pharmacology of DMZ, both what is given in the text and in outside sources. Can we get any clues from another deadly substance James invented, The Entertainment? When his ghost visits Gately in the hospital, James reveals that he created The Entertainment to help Hal climb out of his inner pit of solipsism, but given its addictive, debilitating effects it's hard to imagine how The Entertainment could have ever been beneficial. Likewise, how can the DMZ, which seems just as incapacitating, be used to treat Hal's state of inner decay? One possible answer can be found in the rumors of a cure to The Entertainment, the anti-Entertainment as it's called. Note that this object is never found in the book, but it's theorized to exist. Could the DMZ actually be this very anti-Entertainment? Or something like it? An anti-drug perhaps? If addiction is predicated on the basis of pleasure, then what do we make of a substance like DMZ that is neither addicting nor pleasurable? It's hardly entertaining. So couldn't we call DMZ a type of anti-Entertainment, a kind of anti-drug? What though does an anti-drug do? As a useful analogy, we might look at another odd technology James invented, one called annular fusion. It's a process that feeds on poisons, creating energy and growth from the literal garbage and toxins found in the Great Concavity, a hyper-fertile wasteland. An anti-drug like DMZ would be one that, by a similar analogy, treats cancer "by giving the cancer cells themselves cancer." With DMZ, the infection becomes its own cure.

Although DMZ is an infectious mold, it is also an agent of change, a fertilizer of the soul. As mentioned previously, DMZ is a mold that grows on another mold, possibly the same mold Hal ate as a child. This connection is important—does DMZ have a relationship to mold like a vaccine does to a virus? If the initial mold led to a state of inner rot in Hal, then could the DMZ have somehow healed him, spurring a new phase of inner growth? Molds are the great recyclers of nature, bringing life from death. They can be poisonous, but they can also be refined into drugs with healing properties. I suggest that DMZ is both: a poisonous drug and a healing pharmacological substance. In fact, the etymology of the word *pharmacology* comes from a Greek term, *Pharmakón*. *Pharmakón* in Greek means both poison and cure, and this double meaning is still evident today in our definition of drugs: they can kill, but they can also heal.

DMZ's ability to heal is connected to its capacity to transform the individual, and these are both connected to its effect on the perception of time. There is abundant evidence in both the descriptions of what happens to Hal's sense of time and the list of DMZ's effects on temporality to establish DMZ as the prime catalyst of Hal's transformation. The effects of DMZ are described as "*temporally*-cerebral [...] whereby the ingester perceives his relation to the ordinary flow of time as radically [...] altered" (170). Immediately after brushing his teeth, the effects of DMZ on time begin to distort Hal's perception of reality. Hal notices the digital clock in the bathroom, and the display reads: 11-18EST0456. It is one of the rare moments within the narrative in which the time of day is noted, even though Wallace makes consistent use of time and dates as structural devices to mark chapter breaks, and, noticeably, the time Hal sees is wrong; earlier, in the chapter heading, Wallace had established the date as November 20th. Now, it's certainly possible that this discrepancy is just an error on Wallace's part, but what if it's not a mistake? Is it possible that Hal's own perception of time has begun to shift because of the DMZ? There is more evidence of this. After leaving the bathroom, Hal experiences déjà-vu, the sense that he "had spent lifetimes just here" (897). Hal's temporal rift here mirrors the breakdown of the book's entire timeline, which will fracture and loop back in on itself, coming to a close not in the text's ending words but in the first actual 17 pages of the novel. Which is one way of saying that Hal's end is also a beginning. DMZ's ability to disrupt the passage of time ties into the novel's abundant time-related themes such as growth, decay, the cycle of addiction and sobriety, and of course the possibility of transformation.

The capacity of DMZ to loosen one's grip on time resembles the ability of psychedelics in general to alter the perception of reality. One interesting note in this regard is that out of the wide assortment of recreational drugs, psychedelics are among the least addictive and harmful, and are even considered by some to have beneficial effects like increasing one's state of consciousness and provoking inner growth. In fact, LSD was once used experimentally to treat alcoholics as part of AA. DMZ's status as a psychedelic might be taken to show that, although technically a drug, it might be more helpful than harmful to Hal.

Another salient thing of note about DMZ is that while it resembles the psychedelic class of drugs it is nonetheless an entirely fictional substance.

This is especially interesting in a text displaying a copious amount of detailed, technical data on virtually every other pharmaceutical substance in existence. So why did Wallace feel the need to invent this new drug, DMZ? What is it supposed to be on a pharmacological level, if anything? Earlier we discussed that DMZ is a mixture of two notable psychedelic drugs, LSD and tryptamine-containing mushrooms. But Wallace leaves out textual mention of one other very interesting substance from this same class of drugs: a lesser-known compound called DMT. DMT's full name is N,N-Dimethyltryptamine, and I'll refer to it this way so as not to confuse it with the fictional DMZ. As I'll show, DMZ shares not only a similar name with dimethaltryptamine, but also a similar set of effects. For example, dimethyltryptamine produces an altered state of mind with an uncanny resemblance to DMZ and The Entertainment, like them unleashing a flood of photo-realistic images that completely absorbs the user. Used traditionally in Amazonian shamanism, the visions produced by dimethyltryptamine have actually been compared to watching a film! I will finish this paper by looking at some of the other similarities between DMZ and dimethyltryptamine, as this additional pharmacological context can aid our reading of the role of DMZ in Hal's transformation.

Here for example is one connection between DMZ and dimethyltryptamine that gives more credibility to the idea that James used the DMZ to cure Hal of his emptiness. Dimethaltryptamine has been used as a traditional medicine for millennia by Amazonian shamans, part of a brew still known and used today called ayahuasca. However, like DMZ, the actual shamanistic healing via administration of ayahuasca is hardly a pleasurable one: It's called *la purga*, the purge, and usually involves copious amounts of vomiting. Just as addiction in the novel has been shown as infection from without, the purging that comes from ayahuasca is characterized as a cleansing from within that literally pushes infection back outside the body. Hal stands in need of a similar purging experience, and he gets this from the DMZ, whose effects, if hopefully beneficial in the long-term, are extremely harrowing and painful in the short-term.

While just ascribing DMZ some mystic potency as a healing agent might be a simple enough way to explain how it works, I believe that DMZ is more accurately seen as a kind of recursive self-communication device that lets Hal integrate other voices into his own. It's suggested that James's ghost uses the DMZ in this way so that he can interface with Hal, something he failed to do while alive. There is further support that DMZ functions as a nonverbal communication device if we look at how real-world psychedelics have traditionally been used in this manner. The DMT in ayahuasca is used not only as a healing tool but also as a method for shamans to commune with the spirits, especially the spirits of their own dead ancestors. It continues to be used this way today: the writer William Burroughs actually sought it out for its rumored telepathic powers. We see an example of telepathic communication when James's ghost "speaks" to Gately in the hospital via Gately's own thoughts. Out of their dialog one voice emerges, a sort of hybridization born from the mingling of their consciousnesses. Presumably James doesn't need the DMZ to speak with Gately because, compared to Hal, Gately is much more capable of listening and self-reflection.

James however does need to use the DMZ to put Hal in the right frame of mind to converse with him. The DMZ quiets the external buzz of noise and lets Hal finally hear the voices deep in his mind. The word psychedelic comes from the Greek roots, *psykhe*, meaning "soul," "mind," or "spirit," and *deloun*, which is a verb meaning to "make visible, reveal." Psychedelic then means "mind-revealing," and this is essentially what we're witnessing in Hal: He's getting to know his own mind, his real inner self. As the drug kicks in, Hal becomes fully immobilized, like Gately in his hospital bed a perfect audience to commune with his deepest thoughts. At this point in the novel, Hal's point-of-view switches from a 3rd to a 1st-person perspective, and the switch from the 3rd-person "he" to the 1st-person "I" makes Hal into a character who now truly owns his narrative. It is telling that this is essentially where we leave Hal at the book's end, alone on the floor with just his thoughts for company for perhaps the first real time in his life.

Of course, they're not just his thoughts. If this theory about DMZ acting as a communication device with his father is true, then they're also James's thoughts. Does this invalidate Hal's self-discovery? What do we make of this paradox—let's call it the paradox of language—because we all speak with a voice not entirely our own. In the same way, James's voice must become Hal's own, the without becoming the within. Because up until now, Hal has lacked the inner resources to find his voice. His life has been molded by exterior forces—the Moms, E.T.A., drugs—that left him feeling empty inside, devoid of self-meaning. Of course, you can't find your inner voice unless you listen to someone else. Language must be shared or we wind up sharing Hal's muted fate. So James must communicate with Hal without actually speaking to him. Hal needs to internalize an external world and claim it for his own. He must rely on his own inner substance but not become dependent on another empty substance of choice. And this is the marvelous thing about language: just as mold is a transformer of waste into life, language is a recycling process through which the old becomes new again.

Perhaps this is why Hal needs to be given a non-addictive, anti-drug like DMZ by a ghost. He *must* not know that his transformation has come from something or someone else if he is to truly find his own voice. On a narrative level, this is also why the DMZ goes missing and the source of

Hal's transformation is left unresolved. We must fill in the gaps for ourselves and come up with our own unique solutions. This too is why Hal's cure, DMZ, must be a fictional, invented substance, even though it is based on real pharmacological models like dimethyltryptamine. Like language it comes from shared roots, but ultimately it must be readopted into is own, new form. In this way, DMZ gestures at the possibility of change. It ends in a Z, the very limits of the alphabet, because it's invoking a language that's yet to be spoken.

Interestingly, dimethyltryptamine is the only psychedelic compound produced endogenously in the human body. In other words, while capable of extraordinarily powerful visionary experiences when taken as a drug, it is also always present in the human nervous system, albeit in very trace amounts. Couldn't we say the same thing about the DMZ, which comes from the mold that Hal ate as a child? In a very real sense, Hal has always had the biological roots of this substance within him, but he also needed it introduced from an exterior source, as an anti-drug, to complete his inner transformation and cure him of his infection from the mold. While the native biological function of dimethaltryptamine is unknown, it is theorized to relate to unexplained phenomena like dreams, consciousness, and language. Perhaps because of this it's been dubbed "the spirit molecule." And isn't Hal's dilemma in a sense the loss and discovery of his own human spirit? If so, then James's plan to drug Hal with the DMZ is a success. As his story ends, despite seeming mute to the outside world, Hal finally feels fully alive. He declares triumphantly in his own inner voice, "I am […] I'm not machine. I feel and believe! […] Try to listen […] There is nothing wrong. […] I'm in here." And although the words don't come out at first, Hal's transformation ends on a promising note as he is invited to speak and share his story. This is why Hal's newfound silence at the end of the novel doesn't worry me. Like any infant, Hal *will* learn to speak, with a voice all his own.

Digital Intimacy: Art, Twitter, and DFW's *Infinite Jest*
Corrie Baldauf

Corrie Baldauf
Only Only: Phase 2 of the Infinite Jest *Project*
Image Courtesy of PD Rearick

Two people hear the clip of their laptops close at the same time. One is in Maine, and one is in Detroit (I'll share, this one is me). While these two individuals are separated by a number of miles, they experience a virtual closeness that digitally connects them.

- - -

This isn't quite a chicken or egg story. David Foster Wallace's *Infinite Jest* came first. It was published in 1996. Twitter was founded ten years later, in 2006.

This is a story as to how reading *Infinite Jest* meshed with social media and became *Digital Intimacy*.

- - -

I took my good time to consider anything social media related. In fact, I actively refrained from participating. I believed it would encroach on my time with friends and my time making art. To be honest, the risk of adding another form of *compulsion* to my life was also a concern.

A little over a year ago, I decided to try social media and coincidentally started reading *Infinite Jest* by David Foster Wallace. Two congruous habits began. From where I was standing, I had no idea that these habits would become related rituals.

I chose one of the briefest of social media forms: Twitter. Turns out that mixing Twitter with *Infinite Jest* and art has made for an experience I am really enjoying.

- - -

Pleasure is a consistently slaughtered experience for the characters in *Infinite Jest*. Each person is questing for happiness through *compulsion* or *addiction*. No one is excluded.

Tasks become habits. *Habits* become rituals. *Rituals* become obsessions. *Obsessions* become compulsion. *Compulsion* becomes addiction.

Amanda Thatch (artist) and Rosie Sharp (art critic and artist) repeatedly described the necessity for me, personally, to read *Infinite Jest*. It started as a *task* with reason and expectation. Both are avid readers, so the chance to have something hand-picked by either of them was a treat.

When I started reading *Infinite Jest*, I had to admit I had been too proud of my animus, or inner 'masculine,' as prescribed by the Midwest. There was such a stench of machismo something in those first seventy-six pages that I couldn't take it.

So I set it down.

Around the same time, I came across a package of Semikolon color tabs at a Blick art store. I used to think of color tabs as this generation's version of highlighters—no longer! It was a relatively exciting find for me. As in, something that I thought often about. I could picture the tabs when I was away from them and imagine all the possible things I could do with this 12-color pack of tabs. I was so overwhelmed by their possibility that I left them untouched.

Both *Infinite Jest* and the book of color tabs sat in my bedroom the way unexciting items like socks or flip-flops sit in a bedroom.

- - -

I picked up *Blind Assassin* by Margaret Atwood, which I need to point out was gifted to me in the same handful as *Infinite Jest*. Thank you, Amanda Thatch.

I immediately compared *Blind Assassin* with my attempt to read *Infinite Jest* and was initially struck by two major comparisons:

1) *Blind Assassin* is a smaller commitment; a date versus a relationship.

2) The main characters in *Blind Assassin* are biological sisters. The main characters in *Infinite Jest* are brothers, brothers of all kinds.

One of the characters in *Blind Assassin* is obsessed with describing other characters she admires based on the color and cloth they wear. The level of detail seems far too personal to be fabricated. The author's voice shines through the narration at these moments.

I remembered that small book of color tabs, all 12 colors, and continued reading *Blind Assassin* to completion.

- - -

Why not try to read *Infinite Jest* again? I remembered that the book opens with several color references. Well, three colors. I started listing the colors in my notes:

Brown

"I am in here" (Wallace 3).

yellow

White

White

White

White

yellow

Yellow seemed less of an innocent color sitting in a list and more of an overt throw-up-in-your-mouth dose of racism.

No matter how small, it is an exciting moment when an object of interest to me is matched with a purpose. I really thought that noting the color references would be the impetus that would keep me focused on reading *Infinite Jest*. It worked.

It was a realization that may have saved me a great deal of pain when I was struggling through western education. I have an unfortunate number of books whose marginalia ends in the first pages. You know—the pages that you have to work carefully to hold open because they haven't amassed enough weight to hold themselves down. I fondly joke with students about this in classes I teach. I purposely show them copies of my undergrad texts so that they see where my notes started and ended.

No one has an attention span for everything, and this attention shifts and changes with experience. I think I proved this to myself with the *Infinite Jest* color tab project.

I read the book through, enjoying more than cringing, tracking each reference to color.

Then, I decided to read it again.

This time I had room (mentally) to track each reference to color along with the subject each described. I kept track of the colors, their subjects, and the real time aspect of my recording in email drafts. As I read, every hundred pages, I sent an email to myself—as a digital method of stamping each section of color and subject references with a date and time.

I began to refer to the color-tabbed paperbacks as the *Infinite Jest* Project. It became evident that I was transforming one of my deficits—a frequent inability to focus—into art.

- - -

I started posting to Twitter what I could gather as a brief overview of the stories and people in *Infinite Jest* as short lists of specific colors and subjects (figure 2).

Corrie
@CorrieBaldauf

#OnlyOnly #Phase2 of the #InfiniteJest project. black specks, mask's green strings, golden goose's blackmail p 1-800

Figure 2
Corrie Baldauf
Only Only: Phase 2 of the Infinite Jest *Project*
Image Courtesy of PD Rearick

As I was pretty brand spanking new to all things David Foster Wallace and all things Twitter, I was surprised by the responsiveness Wallace readers had to the *Infinite Jest* Project. There is a visceral moment in Wallace's *Infinite Jest* that comes to mind. It was not unlike being in a highchair and having a loved one slap you on the back so hard that you spit a green gummy bear into the fireplace. It is volatile terrain, and I worked to not get swept up in it in an *obsessed* way.

While maintaining a high level of objectivity about Wallace and Wallace fans, I managed to meet several fascinating people—all because Rosie Sharp posted the first image of the *Infinite Jest* Project on Twitter. Without knowing Wallace, I can comfortably refer to him as a friend maker. Let me emphasize that I am saying the two words: friend maker, not friend singularly. However, pairing the reading of his writing with conversations on Twitter is more intriguing on the conversation front than all other art projects I have completed to date. The conversations do in fact hold a level of transformation that I would normally only associate with the actual process of making the art.

In my second read of *Infinite Jest*, I re-found a quote that helped clarify why Wallace's writing reminds me of my short stint with social media. He describes people's habits, compulsions, and addictions in relation to a media driven enterprise called *The Entertainment*. In this quote he succinctly embodies the sentiment of *The Entertainment*, describing it as an "HD screen set atop the cartridge viewer chassis on its fold-out support like a loved one's photo" (Wallace 1055).

Wow. In the nineties, through *Infinite Jest*, Wallace imagined something not unlike my laptop or yours, or someone's iPad. A term came to mind, in an attempt to qualify what was happening with my reading project that became art and fodder for conversations on Twitter.

Digital Intimacy. I define this term as the experience of finding a connection to people we have not met in person, mainly through language, and viewed on a lit screen that has the same tilt as a printed photograph of someone we know well.

Digital Intimacy is an online language, communicated as worded stories that introduce the writer and transform into moving, living images in the reader's mind. The reader's mind experiences the same reactions to the arrangement of words as it does to the arrangement of being touched, both physically and metaphorically.

The 140-character structure of a tweet omits some of people's tics and mannerisms and, at the same time, reveals their qualities more readily than would happen in person.

Sam Potts is a designer, teacher, and cyclist (@sampotts). Sam made a diagram charting all the characters and their relationships in *Infinite Jest* (figure 3).

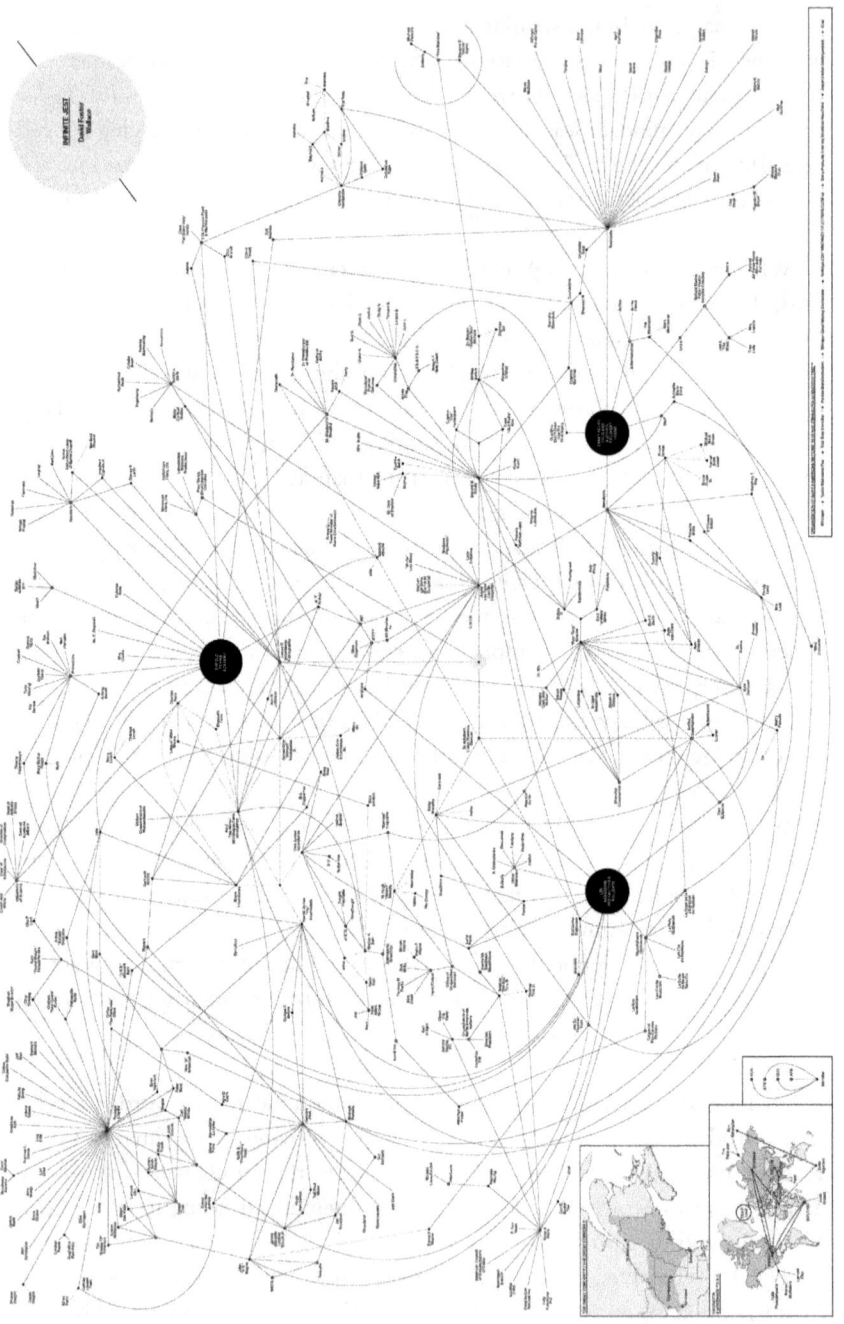

Figure 3
Sam Potts
Infinite Jest diagram, 2010
Image Courtesy of Sam Potts
Learn more about the project at http://sampottsinc.com/ij/

Figure 4
Sam Potts
Infinite Jest buttons
Image Courtesy of Sam Potts

This past summer we did a barter after I posted a quote from the book. Sam had pins with the quote and sent them to me (figure 4). I added color flags to one and sent it back. He hung it in a palm tree (figure 5), which freaked out the archivist in me (in a good way).

Figure 5
Sam Potts and Corrie Baldauf
Infinite Jest, buttons with color tabs
Image Courtesy of Sam Potts

Sam also introduced me to Nick Maniatis, describing him as a pillar and a major supporter in the making of the *Infinite Jest Diagram* poster. My interest was piqued.

Nick, owner of the David Foster Wallace news and resource site[1] (@nick_maniatis), and I started a cross continent conversation on all things Wallace and the projects these things (writing, art, connections between Wallace readers) have inspired. I noticed that he was careful when alluding to Wallace's waking existence. This made a lot of sense to me; Wallace is dead. I have found that when I talk about people in my life that are no longer alive, it is far more grounding to be careful about over-embellishing a dead person's existence.

One day I came across a two-page rainbow-colored spread labeled as Wallace's highlighting. It took me a over a year to get a little *obsessed* about seeing a trace of Wallace that wasn't mass-produced. Excitedly, I asked Nick if he knew about it. He explained the highlighting was misappropriated and was not Wallace's at all. I had to roll my eyes at myself when I lost objectivity. I've learned my lesson.

I have also been in conversation with Christine Zoe Palau, reader and accordion player (@femecovert). She has in fact filled her own copy of *Infinite Jest* with "sign here" stickers. Our conversations are motivating and filled with comic relief. This meant a lot while I worked through color tabbing my second copy of *Infinite Jest*. Christine has sincere energy and a great sense of humor. When looking at a side view of my stacked copies of *Infinite Jest*, she found Lincoln's face in the color tabs. She then retracted and said that it was actually Obama or Papa Smurf she saw. On the sentiment of *Digital Intimacy* she described that images of the books make her "feel all warm and fuzzy."

People's nostalgia for the book, and the conversations that images of the book inspire, is what this project is all about.

Josh Roiland, journalist and professor (@JoshRoiland), has two copies of *Infinite Jest* donning the center of his bookshelf, or should we call it his Twitter banner? It's both. When looking closely, one will also find his Dachshund, Marshall, seated among the books on the same shelf.

Josh has been an emphatic supporter of the project. I have started to think of him as a friend that I look forward to talking with. His research focuses on Wallace's nonfiction, which seems to mesh well with learning to understand how this art project has become just as much about the real-life conversations as the making of the art itself. Josh describes Twitter as "such an interesting, strange thing." Count on Josh to back his support with specific references. He once mentioned Tom Junod—who said, "It really is a meritocracy, that if you do good, interesting work it will find an audience."—to emphasize his interest in the *Infinite Jest* Project.

Closeness finds its way into unexpected places, like say, in a handout, an email, or a tweet. I am finding strains of *digital intimacy* everywhere I type. *Digital intimacy* is a closeness that is experienced without the presence of body language. Comfort and familiarity are still reached, even without physical presence.

And still, these descriptions do not fold or fit neatly into a sock drawer. There are many difficult aspects of *digital intimacy* that I am learning about and realizing. *Digital intimacy* holds a shield to actual intimacy in the way that most long distance relationships do. In spite of the bright glow that projects from *digital intimacy's* screens of communication, it comes with inherent perceptual blackouts. This feels like running into a sequence of walls, unless these darkened moments come with a warning. In reflection, I prefer to be thankful that it is also these inhibitors in *digital intimacy* that help me access more openness to the unknown aspects of the people around me. It is the distance between people I've conversed with, and their openness, that makes risks more possible.

Works Cited

Wallace, David Foster. *Infinite Jest*. New York: Little, Brown and Company, 1996. Print.

"*Infinite Jest*: A Diagram." *sampottsinc*. Sam Potts, 2010. Web. 01 Aug 2010.[1]

[1] http://www.thehowlingfantods.com/dfw/

The Addiction Spectrum: An Analysis of the Three Branches of Addiction in DFW's *Infinite Jest*
Emily Spalding

Positioned in the middle of a room is a cage. Person #1 enters the cage and a key is handed to him. He glances at it, twists it around in his hand, and aggressively throws it outside the barred confinement. Person #2 enters the cage and a key is handed to him. He looks at it with a blank stare and, in his catatonic state, drops it. Person #3 enters the cage and a key is handed to him. After analyzing the details of the key, he maneuvers his arm between two bars and frees the lock.

David Foster Wallace once stated, "in the day-to day trenches of adult life, there is actually no such thing as atheism. There is no such thing as not worshipping. Everybody worships. The only choice we get is what to worship. And the compelling reason for maybe choosing some sort of god or spiritual-type thing to worship is that…anything else you worship will eat you alive" (Kenyon). In *Infinite Jest*, Wallace both intra- and extra-textually stresses the necessity for finding one's addicere, something to which one dedicates his entire life. His individual worship, his entertainment. However, a thin line exists to separate the two sides of this dedication. On one side of this line is worship at its extremity, which can be identified when the addict becomes his addiction. Residing on the other side is a dangerous form of apathy, one that removes any will to continue living. Ultimately, the line serves as a middle ground that is the ideal place for worship. However, as Wallace illustrates in *Infinite Jest*, it is nearly impossible to reach this point. Characters in the novel struggle tremendously with their personal forms of addiction and entertainment, whether it be tennis, drugs, or film, while others strive for an apathetic life.[1] The reader witnesses almost all of the characters lose grip on some facet of their lives to their addictions, and this tragic nature of the characters' fates allows Wallace to exemplify the three branches of addiction on the "Addiction Spectrum."

1   For the sake of this essay, addiction refers to any kind of entertainment which one is obsessed with past the point of normality.

The first branch of addiction occurs when an individual is so attached to his personal entertainment that the addiction overtakes every emotional and physical realm. For example, Wallace describes Joelle Van Dyne as being "at the end of her rope and preparing to hang from it" at Molly Notkin's party because she has "lost the ability to lie to herself about being able to quit [her addiction], or even about enjoying it...it no longer delimits and fills the hole" (219, 222). Now at the point in her drug addiction where she is wholly her addiction, Joelle decides to end her life via suicide, a turn that provides Wallace with one of his most vivid descriptions: "[Joelle] is knelt vomiting over the lip of the cool blue tub...vomiting muddy juice and blue smoke and dots of mercuric red" (240). Wallace writes a similar situation when Gately and Fackelmann embark on their infamous drug binge. Wallace depicts them as "getting off and eating...when they could find their mouths with their hands, moving like men deep under water, heads wobbling on strengthless necks, the empty room's ceiling sky-blue and bulging" and "wet[ting] [their] pants" (935-6). Through these two brutal, eye-opening[2], and dramatic images of addiction, Wallace shows that personal sacrifice is just one of the many prices of addiction and entertainment. The unsettling tone associated with these situations stems from the idea that, even though the characters no longer find pleasure in their addictions, their personal forms of unshakeable entertainments have led them to be completely trapped in souls, minds, and bodies that no longer belong to them.

However extreme the Joelle, Gately, and Fackelmann scenes are, it is important to note that Wallace seldom lets these addicts die. The route of death is too simple, or perhaps too obvious, for the characters. That is because, by electing to die at the hands of most immediate effects of their addictions, the characters are freed from completing emotional arcs. Therefore, Wallace forces the characters to break, struggle, admit defeat, all in order to work through difficulties of their respective addictions. Even then, these characters may not make it through life at the novel's close, but they will still have endured a full emotional journey. As for the characters who pass this extreme test, like Gately, addiction still maintains its presence. Gately's survival attests to the residual effects of addiction; even though he is clean when he is in the hospital, he fears that he will be exposed to drugs again, thus justifying his decision to fight through his wounds sans painkillers of any kind. Wallace presents the nature of addiction as far from ephemeral, proving it to be a lingering and tempting force possessing an incredible amount of power over the addict, no matter how "clean" the addict may be.

Another division of addiction Wallace explores is that of when addicts experience a state of complete acedia. This refusal to invest in any aspect of

---

2   Fackelmann pun intended here.

life appears most dramatically through Hal's friend Pemulis, who declares that Hal "can only quit the Bob if [he] move[s] onward and up to something else… It doesn't have to be harder. It just has to be something" (1065). For Pemulis, "if you're addicted you need it…you lose your mind…you die inside" without the substance, and thus evinces a worldview different from branch one of addiction; he thinks he needs to have something to maintain the ennui of his life though he himself is not his addiction (1056). As he explains to Hal, addiction is just a "word", and any kind of substance will be enough to fuel life's banalities; the only necessity is to have something, regardless of what it is (1065). This style of life is pursued by Pemulis instead of Hal, and it quickly brings on Pemulis's demise. Not only does he get kicked out of Enfield Tennis Academy, but his complete energy expent on his addictions is never directed towards his well-being, but rather towards his emotional destruction. Therefore, neither his exploitation of Avril via pamphlet nor the infamous doorknob incident end his time in the book, but moreover his addiction to not caring about life results in his dismissal from the text.

It is also notable that Wallace disposes of Pemulis's role in the story in an endnote. Pemulis is one of the most salient examples of the second branch of addiction, which, as explained in D.T. Max's *Every Love Story is a Ghost Story*, was the branch that Wallace himself faced most acutely. The strength behind Pemulis's kind of addiction—the addiction to dispassion—is one of the most powerful forms of addiction. It could be argued that Wallace, while writing *Infinite Jest* and overcoming his own addictions, recognized this power and was fearful of it. As a result, he eliminates such an important character in a section of the novel that most readers will miss altogether, minimizing the effects of Pemulis's startling and overwhelming strength and power.

The third and final section of addiction is a balance of the first two branches. It is comparable to the Middle Way of Buddhism, in that there can be a reliance on an entertainment, but there is enough self-control in place that overdose[3] is not a viable option. As Wallace implies in his Kenyon Commencement Speech, achieving and maintaining this balance is incredibly rare: "If you worship money and things, if they are where you tap real meaning in life, then you will never have enough, never feel you have enough…Worship your body and beauty and sexual allure and you will always feel ugly. And when time and age start showing, you will die a million deaths before they finally grieve you" (Kenyon). The only way to find the middle ground is through a presence of truth, or, as Wallace puts it, "the whole trick [to achieving balanced worship] is keeping the truth up front in daily consciousness" (Kenyon). One of the novel's only characters to embody this branch of addiction is Schacht, whom

---

3 Applicable to any kind of entertainment, not just the obvious overdose of drugs

Wallace describes as a person that "doesn't even have to worry about obsessive training…or get sick so often from the physical stress of constant 'drines'" and "like most very large men, he's getting comfortable early with the fact that his place in the world is very small and his real impact on other persons even smaller—which is a big reason he can sometimes forget to finish his portion of a given substance" (267-8). Schacht has found a place in the ennui of life, and he does not need to be excited by an extreme entertainment in order to thrive. Instead, he can act as "one of [those] people who don't need much, much less much more" (268). He is possibly the only character in the book that has found and is satisfied with a middle way, attesting to the rarity of this kind of person in society.

Wallace likens addiction to a cage: "You are behind bars; you are in a cage and can see only bars in every direction. You are in the kind of a hell of a mess that either ends lives or turns them around" (347). Schacht is Person #3 from the opening anecdote of this essay. The inherent difference between Person #3 and Persons #1 and #2 is that, while each one is presented with the same key, Person #3 is the only one with a classification of addiction that will allow him to free himself from the cage. Wallace explains the encaging nature brought on by addiction through the characters of Kate Gompert and James Orin Incandenza. For Kate, the ongoing battle of addiction creeps into every crevice of life, as Wallace reveals when he has her explain her anhedonia and the confining effects that her depression has on her life:

> The so-called 'psychotically depressed' person who tries to kill herself doesn't do so out of quote 'hopelessness' or any abstract conviction that life's assets and debits do not square…The person in whom Its invisible agony reaches a certain unendurable level will kill herself the same way a trapped person will eventually jump from the window of a burning high-rise…when the flames get close enough, falling to death becomes the slightly less terrible of two terrors. It's not desiring the fall; it's terror of the flames (696).

This passage illustrates how the struggles of addiction are primarily personal: no matter how many AA meetings or counseling sessions one attends, one can only realize true progress internally; Wallace has Kate admit that "you'd have to have personally been trapped and felt flames to really understand a terror way beyond falling" (696). As for James Orin Incandenza, Joelle believes his suicide occurred because "he'd stopped being drunk all the time. That killed him. He couldn't take it" (940). Even if Incandenza did not physically drink, the fear of relapsing lurked around him, reviving the trauma associated with his addiction, creating effects similar to Kate Gompert's aforementioned narrative.

There is no way, according to Wallace, to live a life free from the control of something else. Whether it be a tangible or spiritual addiction, life necessitates worship of some form. *Infinite Jest* features characters that experience the extremities of their personal entertainments, and in the end, death is never presented as an acceptable option. While some of the addicts are able to make strides towards a semi tabula rasa through their persistence in overcoming addiction, it is crucial to remember that addiction is ever-present, never leaving absolutely. It is just a matter of how much power the addiction holds in the addict's life, body, mind, and soul that classifies the severity of the addiction. This classification in turn determines where the addict/addiction falls on the Addiction Spectrum.

Works Cited

Wallace, David Foster. *Infinite Jest*. New York: Back Bay Books, 1997. Print.

---. "Transcription of the 2005 Kenyon Commencement Address - May 21, 2005." purdue.edu. N.p., n.d. Web. 14 June 2015. <http://web.ics.purdue.edu/~drkelly/DFWKenyonAddress2005.pdf>.

Identity Beyond Consumer Ethos in DFW's *The Pale King*

Usama Ehsan

Introduction

Previous scholarship and reviews have examined Wallace's *The Pale King* by studying its relationship with the "politics of boredom" (Ralph Clare), "narrative" and "consciousness" (Stephen J. Burn), philosophy and the self (Allard den Dulk), community and narrative (Andrew Warren), humans and computers (Conley Wouters), and taxes and civic responsibility (Marshal Boswell), but none have explored the postmodern individual in light of the culture industry and its dependence on group dynamics such as the Internal Revenue Service ("the systems"), family, and relationships (i.e: boyfriend/girlfriend and/or friendship, co-workers). By exploring the self in relation to group dynamics, I would like to contend that the self in *The Pale King*, the individual identity, can no longer protect and preserve itself, because it is not a coherent and strong force as the modernist thinkers (Kierkegaard, Kafka, and Dostoevsky) once conceived. While the modernist notion of the self found power and strength through alienation and solitude (individualism), David Foster Wallace presents a nuanced version of the postmodernist self, one that finds strength and coherence through a collective. In the postmodern sphere, individual identity or the self tends to be defined as the individual who is unable to become fully aware of his true goal and whose identity is dictated and dependent on a consumer ethos. As a way out of postmodern alienation, David Foster Wallace introduces the group or the collective, which can be defined as partners, family, friends, co-workers, or some type of pluralistic relationship that influences the individual to become strong, coherent, and active in the sense that the individual is able to reach his goal and care for others beyond a consumer ethos.

My paper will (1) provide an overview of the modernist's notion of the self, (2) examine certain characters' development throughout the novel as it pertains to my argument that the postmodernist self is not just alienated and fragmented but consumed by its lack of desire to care for others and by the culture industry of 1980s Peoria, Illinois, and (3) explain how the group dynamics help strengthen these individuals' identities beyond consumer/cultural ethos, an ethos where the importance lies in communication and caring for others.

Philosophy of the Self

In order to understand my focus on the group dynamics relation to the individual in David Foster Wallace's *The Pale King*, I cannot help but begin by introducing the notions of the self in a brief philosophical history as it relates to Wallace's works. The 19th/20th century philosophers Søren Kierkegaard and Friedrich Nietzsche highly praised an individual's experience and identity as a force that could change its environment from inside its own solitude. Kierkegaard writes in his journal, "I must find a truth that is true for me... the idea for which I can live or die," and this idea or ideal provides the self (individual) with strength, power, and an active direction to change the self in society. Nietzsche's nihilistic rejection of truth, morals, values, and religion as a means to "overcome itself" (*Zarathustra II.12*) by destroying and self-overcoming offers a nuanced perspective on Wallace's characters. As characters in the novel chafe against conventions, they ironically experience their individuality in terms of what Wallace calls a "wasteoid," a person who is consumed by the countercultural movement that rejects everything in order to be cool, hip, or likable (fashionable). To further understand why Wallace struggled with the notions of an individual's strength to break out of conformity, his views on the 20th century writers like Franz Kafka and Fyodor Dostoevsky provide an insightful perspective to the importance of individuals' stories. Both existential writers display a profoundly different exploration of the human condition that in Wallace's words meant "What it is to be a human being" (*Consider the Lobster*), where "the horrible struggle to establish a human self results in a self whose humanity is inseparable from the horrific struggles. That our endless and impossible journey toward home is in fact our home" ("Laughing with Kafka" 26). Contrastingly, what is "home" for the characters in the novel, as I will argue later, is being part of a collective that supports the community at large, and what is not "home" is fragmented, alienated, lost, and unable to reach any goals. Furthermore, I would also illustrate that "what it is to be a human being" in the *Pale King* is to communicate and care beyond the individual's selfish desires/actions, to have a sense of "civic virtue" (Wallace, *TPK* 135) "for the good of the nation and not just to advance their own interests" (136).

I will focus my argument on Chris Fogle because I believe that he, individually, embodies the postmodernist's condition of alienation and fragmentation due to the consumerism, capitalism, and (counter) cultural movements, but he also illustrates how a collective entity like the Internal Revenue Service and their group dynamics help repair and reconstruct their identity beyond a consumer ethos and toward "civic virtue."

Chris Fogle: Confessions of an IRS Wiggler

Chris Fogle's chapter in *The Pale King* provides an accurate example of (1) the dominance of consumerism, (2) the ecstasy of increasing capital, and (3) a certain countercultural movement that made the 1960s as a "'free and freeing' period that eventually inspired a childish desire for parental authority" (Boswell 471). All of these issues that stem from the consumerist ethos have fragmented Fogle's sense of self/identity in a postmodern context. David Lyon's *Postmodernity* comments on how the postmodern individual's "values and beliefs seem to lose any sense of coherence, let alone continuity, in the world of consumer choice, multiple media and globalized postmodernity," and this loss results in individuals with the "vertigo of relativity" and the "abyss of uncertainty" that is centered on the "consequence of a world where choice reigns supreme; hesitation, anxiety, and doubt seem to be the price paid for the sense of choice" (77). The postmodern generation's "shift from fate to choice, or from providence to progress, that was supposed to be so liberating, appears to have a darker side, which unveils the further spiral into nihilism," but in this particular chapter, Chris Fogle transforms from a wasteoid/nihilist/hipster to an IRS tax examiner who finds motivation from group dynamics rather than alienation and solitude.

Taking Lyon's commentary and situating it in the context of *The Pale King*, particularly Chris Fogle's chapter on his past and present decision to join the Internal Revenue Systems, exhibits the "vertigo of relativity," the "abyss of uncertainty," and the "darker side" of consumer ethos's effect on fragmenting Fogle's sense of self. The problem with the self in postmodernity is that characters' identities/selves become alienated, or rather they do not have the will to establish a goal or become motivated beyond their self-absorption/consumption. Fogle says that his past before the I.R.S. was essentially an "unmotivated period" (157), where his father referred to it as a lack of "initiative" (156). Fogle characterizes his past "like a piece of paper on the street in the wind, thinking 'Now I think I'll blow this way, now I think I'll blow that way,'" which parallels his decision to "drift for several years, in and out of three different colleges, one of them two different times, and four or five different majors. One of these might have been a minor.... I was pretty much a wasteoid" (165). Again, Lyon's words resonate with Fogle's past because there comes the ultimate "consequence" of "choice," which causes "vertigo...hesitation, anxiety, and doubt." The key word to describe Fogle's past is the notion of a "wasteoid," which he says is a "response to everything [as] 'Whatever'" (156). In addition to the notion of a "wasteoid," Fogle describes himself as "the worst kind of nihilist—the kind who isn't even aware he's a nihilist" (156). The modernist period—specifically Nietzsche's concept of selfhood as an alternative claim to his nihilistic rejection of truth, morality, values, and religion—is essentially the "Will" in human beings, where the "Life itself is Will to Power" (*BGE* 13). However, "the worst kind of nihilist" does not find strength in the period of postmodern alienation, fragmentation, and solitude because of choice and consumerism. One reason for Fogle to characterize it as "the worst" is because there is no coherency and civic virtue in this form of individualism. This form of individualism for Fogle came in the dynamics of "the child trying to sort of passively rebel while still financially tied to the parent" (158), which in chapter nineteen is termed as "liberal individualism" (132). Essentially, the self and its form of individualism occur to Fogle as "the lack-of-direction thing" and "passive" (158), and do not help him strive or reach for anything beyond himself. Fogle's decisions in the past become a maelstrom of events that avoid "the boredom," "the boring and [the] meaningless" (157).

For example, on discussing his past he remembers "Ritalin versus Ritadex, Cylert and Obetrol…John Travolta, disco fever…'Fonz'…. Actually preferring…Tang to real orange juice…. Smoking pot after school and then watching TV and eating Tang out of the jar with a finger.… Sitting there with my wasteoid friends" (160). He comments that in this phase of his life he "was dead or asleep without even being aware of it." In this example, the reader understands that his consumption of Tang and marijuana while watching TV in his father's living room illustrates that he has no concept of caring beyond himself. To care means to pay "serious attention or consideration applied to doing something correctly or to avoid damage or risk,"[1] but Fogle does not seem to pay any close attention to the consequences of his recreational leisure time.

The chapter before Fogle (ch. 19) expresses a debate about the concept of civics and taxes as it pertains to the new selfish generation in the US. The issue with Chris Fogle and other characters in this novel, as one character says, is that "We don't think of ourselves as citizens—parts of something larger to which we have profound responsibilities" (132). The second broad arc of the novel—"Being individual vs. being part of larger things—paying taxes, being 'lone gun' in IRS vs. team player" (547)—clearly resonates in chapter nineteen. In relation to my argument, another character (in ch. 19) says that Fogle's generation is where "America's starting to decline into decadence and selfish individualism—the Me generation" (134). Fogle's past, as he and his father would describe it, is being the "conformist…a hypocrite, a 'rebel' who really just sponged off of society in the form of his parents" (167). Just as Fogle's father is strict and adamant about him finishing school and being responsible, the characters in chapter nineteen suggest that the people in the U.S. "expect the government to be the parent that takes away the dangerous toy" (140), but it is Fogle and other characters' decisions and selfishness that "We abdicate

---

1   "Care." *New Oxford English Dictionary*. Web. 14 Apr. 2015

our civic responsibilities to the government," or to parents, keeping the names unknown and talking about "We the government" or "We…the citizens" (132). "We" functions linguistically as a non-referent pronoun that makes the reader assume that he/she is included in the "We," yet the chapters in *The Pale King* expose the individual character's past and present in relation to their group dynamics. Furthermore, chapter nineteen exemplifies the issues Fogle and his generation are dealing with: "the corporations will be able to represent consumption-patterns as the way to break out—use this type of calculator… wear this type of shoe because everyone else is wearing conformist shoes" (148). Eventually, "Voting'll be unhip," as one character says, and in relation to Fogle his sense of nihilism or "wasteoid" shows that his self in postmodernity is alienated and fragmented to the point where he cannot decipher what is being sold for his benefit or for capitalist gains/consumerism. Similarly, the concept of voting, in and of itself, revolves around the concept of civics, but Fogle says: "I don't think I voted. The truth is that I don't remember if I voted or not…. Got distracted somehow and didn't get around to it" (166). To a certain extent, selfish interests and consumerism as it relates to corporations marketing to Fogle's generation creates an inimical situation for Fogle's identity, wherein which his wasteoid-ness has taken over his responsibility to his parents and country. An example of this type of nonconformist delusion is Fogle's roommate, who "blatantly rationalized his selling of drugs as a form of social rebellion instead of just pure capitalism" (166). Fogle further adds that he "knew he (the roommate) was a total conformist to the late-seventies standards of so-called nonconformity…but this kind of blatant projection and displacement was part of the nihilist hypocrisy of the whole period" (166). Fogle's comment on "the nihilist hypocrisy of the whole period" ironically includes him, a character who in "1975 or 76', shav[ed] off just one sideburn…believing the one sideburn made [him] a nonconformist" (163). Charles Jencks, an American architect who has written history books on modernism and post-modernism, describes "the Post-Modern Age" as "a time of incessant choosing. It's an era when no orthodoxy can be adopted without self-consciousness and irony" (7). Wallace's chapter on Fogle illustrates that postmodernity embodies a culture of delusion and self-consumption for profits: an identity based merely on a consumer ethos, whose decisions avoid responsibility and civics for selfish desires/goals. The first broad arc of the novel deals with "awareness" and "boredom," and as we can see in this earlier part of Fogle's chapter, the anxiety of consumerist ethos has rendered the self unable to establish any clear and distinct goals. Furthermore, the first broad arc, an outline of how certain characters in the novel deal with boredom and anxiety, illustrates that Fogle's life before the "Systems (I.R.S.)" was incongruent, particularly because he had no means of "paying attention" and overcoming "boredom." His identity, as he repeatedly remarks in his ninety-nine page chapter, was "unaware" and "dead." Individually, Fogle cannot help himself, and the modernist notion of solitude as a means to overcome does not happen for him, but coincidentally the death of his father and walking into the wrong classes create a series of events that help shape his identity for the better.

Chris Fogle's chapter illustrates that the self cannot prosper beyond a consumer ethos because his identity is unable to gain the tools and direction needed to find "initiative" (167), but his father's disgust on the "nihilistic scene" (172-3) in the living room, the use of Obetrol, his father's death, the tax accounting class he mistakenly walks in, and the Internal Revenue Service illustrate that the group dynamics help repair/renew the self through sacrificing the freedom of being a wasteoid. Fogle narrates that "things began to get much more vivid, focused, and concrete in 1978" (175) because this was the year he "'found himself' or 'put away childish things' and began the process of developing some initiative and direction...which led to [him] joining the Service" (174). What was this change? Rather how did this change happen, and what was the catalyst that led to Fogle's "developing some initiative and direction"? Fogle's father's death indirectly "connected to [his] choice of the IRS as a career" (174). Before his father's death, one other incident shaped his understanding of how his actions reflected his identity changing. Fogle and his friends are drinking beer, smoking pot, watching TV, and trashing the living room, and Fogle's father unexpectedly comes home from work early; he takes a look at his living room and in anger says, "*Look on my works, ye mighty, and despair!*," a direct reference to Victor Frankenstein's problem with the Creature, then goes up the stairs, does not slam the door, and quietly goes into the bedroom (172). For the first time, Fogle imagined how he must have looked to his father: "like a spoiled little selfish child." Furthermore, it was also the first time Fogle "remember[ed] feeling like shit," not because of the drugs, but because there was this feeling of caring beyond himself, of merely putting himself in his father's shoes and not just seeing but feeling his "disgust" (173). In relation to my argument, the group dynamics involved here in repairing and renewing Fogle's self/identity are his father's disgust that made him realize he was wasting his life. There is no way that Fogle could have found this insight through the modernist's notion of solitude, but rather through the Wallacian notion of "paying attention" and being part of "the larger things (second broad arc)" (547). Furthermore, what also shaped Fogle to join the Service ("Systems") was what he called "*Obetrolling,*" (183) a drug which suppresses appetite but makes one feel that they are aware of everything. "Obetrolling" made Fogle "feel alive," but he also says, "It felt like I actually *owned* myself. Instead of renting or whatever" (188). In a consumer society, the clothes, food, music, and everything we consume through the senses creates an inimical situation for the self because it causes a sense of fragmentation, where the body is "rented" for brands and capitalism. David Lyon writes that "if postmodernity means anything, it means the consumer society" (88), and in this part of Fogle's life, he is working to go beyond the consumer ethos. Jean Baudrillard, a French sociologist, philosopher, cultural theorist, and political commentator, says that postmodernity affects individual identity because "it is the end of interiority and intimacy" (*The Ecstasy of Communication*), but with Obetrol and his father's disgust, Fogle is reclaiming his inner self, or rather his world of "interiority." In addition, these previous events, Fogle says, "had something to do paying attention and the ability to choose what I paid attention to, and to be aware of that choice, the fact that it's a choice" (189), rather than an automatic consumption of capitalistic influence. Another incident that indirectly related to Fogle having direction in his life was the death of his father while Christmas shopping. Fogle tried to catch up to his father on the train's platform, but his father was closer to the train. As his father moved past two large Hispanic shoppers' bags, he used his hands to stop the train's door from closing, but the train's door closed with his arm halfway between the doors. The train started moving and killed him. Fogle describes the scene: "many of these people were also holding numerous small, subdivided packages and individually purchased bags, many of these could be seen flying up in the air…that it was somehow spurting or raining consumer goods" (204). Lyon's concept of "vertigo" as a consequence of postmodernism and consumerism as a way of life can be interpreted as the cause of his father's death. His father died because there were too many people, which was due in part to the character' shopping. Ironically, Wallace portrays the death of the father amongst the "raining of consumer goods" to show how no one on the train's platform is paying attention or even aware of the train pulling a man towards his death. This type of addiction to self-interest can be posited as a concept in *The Pale King* that hurts the postmodern individual identity. Fogle's awareness of his father's death helped him in his "changes in priorities and directions" (211). The concept of choice had previously left the individual with the "vertigo of relativity" and the "abyss of uncertainty" that caused "hesitation, anxiety, and doubt" (Lyon 77), but now Fogle's new development through the help of his father and his death made him realize that he is aware and responsible for his choices in life through the group dynamics.

    The Jesuit substitute tax professor also dramatically shifted Fogle's wasteoid lifestyle towards civics and responsibility. Running late to his final exam, Fogle mistakenly walks into a similar but identical room that is lecturing on "Advanced Tax" (232). Mr. Gorton, the professor, left such an impression on Fogle that his lecture forced him to reconcile his wasteoid/nihilist past and move towards caring beyond a consumer ethos. Mr. Gorton exclaims to the whole class and Fogle:

> Gentlemen, here is the truth: Enduring tedium over real time in a confined space is what real courage is. Such endurance is…Heroism…. The truth is that heroism of your childhood entertainment was not true valor. It was theater. Here is the truth—actual heroism receives no ovation, entertains no one. No one queues up to see it. No one is interested. (231)

Upon hearing this, Fogle's sense of self became renewed and his old childish ways were to put to rest. Yet one other thing that illustrates how the group dynamic helped repair/renew Fogle's sense of self is the concept of caring beyond a consumer ethos. The professor's rhetoric adheres and relays the concept of a "hero" that forces students in the classroom to come to terms within themselves. Furthermore, Mr. Gorton emphasizes "Effacement. Sacrifice. Service," and most importantly, "to retain care…about each detail from data…. To attend fully to the interests of the client…. To give oneself to the care of others' money—this is effacement, perdurance, sacrifice, honor, doughtiness, valor" (233). The words used in this part of the Jesuit professor's speech furthers the notion of awareness and caring beyond one's own selfish consumptions. As a consequence to the speech, Fogle "remember[s] having a strong urge to lean over and tie [his] boots' laces" (233). Throughout Fogle's ninety-nine page monologue, the transition from a self-consumed individual halted after he ironically stepped into the wrong room, and when the speech was over, Fogle recalls being in a "strange kind of hyperaware daze, both disorientated and clear" (235). Furthermore, the first thing Fogle does after the speech and during the holidays is get a haircut, research requirements and options for the CPA exam, buy a guidebook to the CPA Exam, get a complete suit, apply to the IRS, and completely change his prospective career to serving others.

In the chapter on Fogle, David Foster Wallace writes about a new kind of postmodern self—one that markedly differs from the modernist self embodied in Kierkegaard, Kafka, and Dostoevsky (which, to summarize, is solitary, alienated, and suffering but which discovers itself in solitude). This new kind of postmodern self is indeed alienated—it is a "wasteoid," as Chris Fogle embodies early on—but it can find a new sense of enduring and vital identity in a group context as part of a collective. In the novel, this collective is embodied in the IRS, a collective whose special quality (and the irony is keenly, constantly noted) is that to work there is so unbearably boring and dull that to profit from being part of it requires real "attentiveness," a heightened awareness to detail (in one's work, surely, but also in one's whole environment) that eventually brings one closer to oneself and others. Fogle's entrance to the IRS is a great example of how Wallacian "attentiveness" can work; it is a world-directed awareness that manages to quiet the self's own needs—to put it simply, *to care*.

Acknowledgment

I wish to thank Dr. Cornel Bonca, Dr. Kelman, and Dr. Martha Webber for their helpful comments on earlier versions of this essay. I am particularly grateful, however, to Dr. Richard Godden and Dr. Michael P. Clark for their patience and guidance in forming the basis of theory in this paper. Lastly, I'd like to thank Natasha Barrett for her motivation, encouragement, and insightful email that helped make this essay possible.

Works Cited

Boswell, Marshall. "Trickle Down Citizenship: Taxes and Civic Responsibility in *The Pale King*." *David Foster Wallace and "The Long Thing": New Essays on the Novels*. New York: Bloomsbury, 2014. 216. Print.

Boswell, Marshall. *David Foster Wallace and "The Long Thing": New Essays on the Novels*. New York: Bloomsbury, 2014. 216. Print.

Burn, Stephen. "'A Paradigm for the Life of Consciousness': Closing Time in *The Pale King*." *Studies in the Novel*, 44.4 (2012): 371-388

Clare, Ralph. "The Politics of Boredom and the Boredom of Politics in David Foster Wallace's *The Pale King*." *Studies in the Novel*, 44.4 (2012): 428-446.

Cohen, Samuel S., and Lee Konstantinou. *The Legacy of David Foster Wallace*. Iowa City: U of Iowa, 2012. Print.

Elderon, S. "The Shaping of Storied Selves in David Foster Wallace's the Pale King." *Critique Studies in Contemporary Fiction*, 55.5 (2014): 508-521.

Freeman, John. "Fallen King: Wallace's Posthumous Novel About a Bureaucratic, Deathly Bored, and Soulless America Reminds Us of His Singular Talent and of What Could Have Been." *Boston Globe*, (2011): C.5.

Harvey, David. *The Condition of Postmodernity: An Enquiry into the Origins of Cultural Change*. Oxford: Blackwell, 1990. Print.

Jenks, Charles. *What is Postmodernism?*. London: Academy Editions, 1989. Print.

Lyon, David. *Postmodernity*. Minneapolis: U of Minnesota, 1999. 77. Print.

McLanahan', Sarah, and Gary Sandefur. *Growing Up With A Single Parent*. Boston: Harvard UP, 1997. *The American Prospect*. Web. 12 June 2015.

Nietzsche, Friedrich. "On Self-Overcoming." *Thus Spoke Zarathustra*. Trans. Walter Kaufmann. New York: Viking Penguin, 1966. 115-16. Print.

Wallace, David F. "Laughing with Kafka." *Harper's Magazine* July 1998: 23-27. Web.

Wallace, David Foster. *The Pale King: An Unfinished Novel*. New York: Back Bay, 2012. Print.

Wallace, David Foster. *This Is Water: Some Thoughts, Delivered on a Significant Occasion about Living a Compassionate Life*. New York: Little, Brown, 2009. Print.

The Man Who Flew Into Space Leaves His Forthcoming Going Away Party Early Thus Putting an Abrupt End to 5.5 Years of "Academic Mobbing"

Jodie Childers

It was a cosmic affair / a subatomic bomb particle party, beware
Dr. Smithson was there / Dr. Wesson III was there,
the entire metaphysed department from Prickly Pear—
It all started when he was promoted.

You see, an interstellar mind must be demoted.
There was a big bang

bang

(the party ended early)
A CV cut short
(He was always in a hurry)
catapulting here / projecting there

I think there was a gun somewhere.

And nobody at the going-away-wine/cheese-party said hi.
And nobody at the funeral-all-you-can-eat-wine/cheese-party said bye.
Faculty wives in one room,
faulty husbands in another.

that night
He said (I need you all to go now)
that night
He said (I need to be alone now)

Perhaps, one day he'll come back down
get off his high jet stream
& fall under ground
[i.e. gravity dot dot dot]

Inscribing Soleas
Alex Bertacchi Passett

a short story about how ignorance is *not* always bliss

"So when we look at *Handcrafted Epyllia*, what do we see? What do we hear from the words?"

Mr. Floy. What a chump.

I'm in my seat, and two fat chicks sandwich me in so hard I feel like I'm going to fuse with the chair. I feel like I have to hurl.

And by that, I'm not just talking about trying not to upchuck last night's takeout between these double-decker slobs.

This class, English 135, Section 5, is trash. Don't want it. Don't need it. The prof, Mr. Floy, calls it Introduction to Narrative Style. It's an afternoon Gen Ed I have no choice but to take. Reading isn't for me. Writing definitely isn't for me. Add on Fatties One and Two clogging the air, material that puts me to sleep, and Mr. Floy with his tacky-ass getups, long hair and stupid jokes, and this whole thing is just repulsive.

"If you haven't already, open to page twenty-nine."

There must be forty, maybe fiftyish students in English 135, Section 5. Most of them are hideous. Everyone flips frantically. Forty, maybe fiftyish sets of hideous hands fingering through slabs of stories in our required text, and here I am sitting, just sitting, because I didn't do the reading.

Everyone's looking at their books, avoiding eye contact. No one wants to speak up.

I hope no one read it. That'd make it easier on me.

"In *Handcrafted Epyllia*, the textbook gives us notes in the margins as to what is going on, but I implore you to go beyond that. Listen to what I'm asking, without the CliffsNotes. What do you all see? How did you interpret the piece?"

No one says a thing.

Ha. Good.

"Anyone? There must be someone ready and willing to guide us along!"

Boy, he is way too enthusiastic.

"Anyone…"

God, I just want a nap.

"Come on, now."

Yeah. Come on now, guys! Talk! Talk about *Handjobbed Godzilla*!

"Bueller? Bueller?"

Oh don't make jokes, you Ben Stein wannabe.

"But seriously now, really, what is it you see? How did the plight of the two main characters make you feel?"

The fuck's a plight?

No one has spoken up yet. Maybe he'll stop trying…

"How about a pop quiz on it?"

Mr. Floy, Mayor Dickwagon, Colonel Munchole, Buzzkill Supreme.

Now the frantic flipping quickens fivefold and two, three, four hands shoot up in the air trying to get his attention.

Suckers, all of them.

"Yes, you? What do you think about it?"

Generic Goon Student takes the floor.

"I felt, uh, bad when it happened."

"Felt bad?" Mr. Floy asks. "Can you be a tidbit more descriptive?"

Can you be a tidbit more of a faggot?

"Um," he stutters. "It was sad, uh, to see it happen when they were, um, the only two people in the whole thing."

"Bingo!" Mr. Floy is still way too excited. "So based on that response, you felt, well, robbed as a reader? Because the commitment you made to the characters in the beginning of the narrative was shattered wholly in the end?"

Generic Goon Student looks like a deer square-on in the headlights. Hope he gets hit.

"Yea, yea…" he sputters out.

They're both faggots.

"Excellent," Mr. Floy continues. "That's why we steer away from vague answers. I like it." He pauses, and I wish he'd just choke on something. "So there's one thought. How about another?"

How about not?

"I really liked it," this girl in the second row says. Her voice is high-pitched and whiny.

"In what way?"

You're yanking teeth, Mr. Floy. Enough with the fucking questions.

"It was tragic, but realistic. It's something I could, like, see happening. Not that I want it to happen, 'cause, like, no, but it could."

"Now that's some selective language! Tragic, but realistic. Yes! We connect with the fictional characters while acknowledging the likelihood of something like this happening. Thank you."

Great. Shrill Broad got one right.

"We'll get more into this later, but *Handcrafted Epyllia*, this short award-winning tale, is something I'd like us all to refer back to as the semester progresses. Being able to relate to the protagonists in such a short story is a huge part of this course. Not to mention the feeling, as a reader, of having the rug swept out from beneath you just when you've gotten situated with the story and immersed yourselves."

This is bananas. What special recipe of Hell am I in?

"You guys may want to take all this down."

A jailbreak of panicky noises erupts again. The page-flipping turns to pen-scribbling, the line-scanning to loose-leaf-ripping, and here I am with zero interest and not a damn clue as to what they're talking about, stuffed between two sweaty female versions of the Hulk and the Stay Puft Marshmallow Man.

No time to call the Ghostbusters to exorcise Mr. Floy, either.

Fuck it.

I stand up, heading for the back door of the lecture hall, and wouldn't it be my luck that Mr. Floy sees me leaving.

"Can you take your seat, Soleas? We're in the middle of a discussion."

I don't say anything. I keep walking.

"Excuse me? Soleas?"

Peppy profs like this make me sick.

I stop, and I tell him that other professors don't halt everything on a dime just because one person is getting up to take a tinkle. Generic Goon Student covers up a laugh. Mr. Floy notices this, probably thinking I'm the class clown now. That I've struck a witty match and now anarchy will burn free.

Man, the Fountain of Sarcasm never runs dry, does it?

"Well I do. I don't mean to be rude, but you're being rude to me. Would you please take your seat?"

I ask him why.

Fatty Two gasps, like I'm a snot-nosed academic blasphemer who just squatted over the Bible and broke the student-teacher code of conduct. Lord, no. Heavens forbid! I talked back.

She should save her breath for the crumbling, half-chomped, coffeecake-flavored cinnamon roll stuffed in her side pocket.

Mr. Floy is unamused. He tilts back away from the lectern, leaning against the wall, spreading his hands on the little ledge for markers and erasers. Probably thinks he looks like a damn Christ figure.

"You haven't read *Handcrafted Epyllia*, Soleas. That's obvious, otherwise you'd understand the gravity of this. What's even more apparent is that you don't seem to recall the part in our syllabus about hecklers in my class."

Another chick sitting along the aisle murmurs to me, telling me to *shut up*, telling me *it's not worth it*.

I tell Mr. Floy no, I don't recall, but I also couldn't give a rat's ass.

Houston, we have Hallelujah.

It's like a tennis match now. Everyone's eyes bounce back and forth from me to Mr. Floy, then to me, then to Mr. Floy.

I don't regret starting this, though. It's intense, probably the highlight of their day.

"This is fun, huh? This a game to you, isn't it Soleas?"

He doesn't sound intimidating. I just wish he'd stop repeating my name, like he's treating me the way negotiators handle hostage-takers.

I tell him it is fun, and that I still have to let loose that piss.

Fifteen-love. Shrill Broad is flabbergasted by my tone. I like it.

"I don't tolerate hecklers, Soleas. You put me on the spot, I'll put you on the spot."

I ask him if he's heckling me now.

Ooh, serve returned.

"You're not getting off easy. We have two classes blocked off this week for *Handcrafted Epyllia*. I specifically carved that out, just to give the structure of this class some wiggle room. You think you're stalling me and ruining my lesson plan, but you're not. We can do this all day. You're just making a fool out of yourself."

Someone whispers to someone else, asking if he can say that.

Now I'm wondering if someone will report him to the university. Or report me.

A lull fogs down onto us. We're at a standoff. I imagine gray quills of clouds overhead, feathering the ceiling tiles. The pale walls and thin, cockroach-brown carpet are our Old Western town. Mr. Floy can be Tuco, and Generic Goon Student can be Angel Eyes. I might as well be Clint Eastwood.

The Good, the Bad, and the I Don't Give A Fuck About Introduction to Narrative Style.

I imagine a quiet tumbleweed rolling past. Mr. Floy doesn't flinch.

"Let's get down to brass tacks then. Let's make this real." Mr. Floy straightens his posture like he's an actor preparing a scene. "You have right around a sixty-two percent in this class, Soleas. That's a low D. Walk out of here and I'll drop it to an F with no opportunities for extra credit."

I hear another gasp, but I tell him I don't care. I tell him grades aren't everything. I tell him to go stuff his extra credit.

No one can believe the roll I'm on right now.

"I've met people like you, Soleas. You don't care about the education you're lucky to have. Your parents must be spoon-feeding you. You don't care about decency. All the while you neglect your studies and disrespect your instructors, coming off as unappreciative and bad-mannered."

I tell him I do care, just not about this class. I'm more of a prob and stats kind of guy.

"I, on the other hand, don't think you care. Not a bit," he counters, hammering his foot down on the word *don't*.

I throw in that his big, fancy-word lines sound like he's trying to cram too much into one pretentious sentence.

Mr. Floy scoffs. His face reddens.

I swear, this is like a captivating, daytime soap to everyone else in the room.

"The statistics major is criticizing the diction of the English professor?" he asks me. I can hear the vinegar sizzling in his throat. "You've got some balls, Soleas."

I tell him that's what his sister said last night.

And just like that, everyone loses the ability to contain themselves. Some boo. Some hoo-hah. A couple goth kids in the back pretend to catcall. Three frat-looking guys pound the backs of their chairs like furious baboons. The rest of my classmates just sit there in what I'd like to think is awe.

I feel like a ringleader. A glorified ringleader, fit with a top hat and pinstripes and all.

Step right up, I think to myself in a booming announcer voice. Welcome to the Big Top! Our main event…The Incorrigible Mr. Floy!

I take a step in his direction and I tell him that I did do some homework, with a crank of emphasis on *some*. Some homework on him. I tell him I looked up floy, and that floy-floy was used in a song once as slang for a venereal disease.

Yeah, that's right. I just called my prof an STD.

You're the herpes of college professors, I shout!

After this performance, I'd like to thank the Academy for what has turned into an unexpectedly magnificent day.

I don't even care what happens next. My temper squelches out of me like thick mud through a narrow drainpipe. All this, coming out of nowhere.

Full disclosure, I think I may be a fun-loving hothead.

Mr. Floy is a fallen gargoyle, perched onto nothing. He doesn't toss a jab of his own back at me. He doesn't move.

He doesn't move…

Doesn't…move…

The fuck? Why isn't he moving?

Then, he shifts towards me like he's on a chessboard.

"No one else would entertain this," he says, his voice like a low engine, rumbling. "Your peers have witnessed this. I can have you expelled. Arrested even, if I wanted to go that far. Or, I can get on with our class."

I sneer at him now.

That's it?

Empty threats?

That's your secret weapon?

Your Crème de la Floy?

You're schooling me with that?

Fuck me, is that rich.

"You win, Soleas. Congrats. You've made your point. Go. Leave."

I turn away from him and chuckle to myself. What a fucking pushover. What a—

"You may want to do a Google search on the author of *Handcrafted Epyllia*, though."

For the life of me, I don't know why I look back, but I do. So I coo at him mockingly, asking him why I should bother.

He parts his hair and locks in on me.

"Because I wrote it, you ingrate little shit."

Immediate silence blankets the lecture hall.

Now, what do you say to that?

I say nothing. Someone whips out their phone and starts videoing.

"Now is as good of a time as any, isn't it, Soleas?"

For what?

I don't understand. I'm dumbstruck.

"In our book, it was originally going to say that *Handcrafted Epyllia*'s author was left anonymous. I would've specifically had the publisher do that when they'd go to print this collection for our class, and then it would've been a surprise for you all.

"But I didn't," he says. "Right there on its title page. There's my name."

My mouth is still shut. I'm thinking that, okay, maybe that's slightly impressive, but it isn't a ruthless mic drop at the end of an extreme rap battle.

Mr. Floy? A thug? Hell no.

Then why am I still silent?

"But you know, maybe it's better, for me at least, that you didn't know. Didn't even open the book. This way, it really speaks to your ignorance, Soleas. And disarms it." Floy almost hisses.

What, I mutter.

"Dude, did you not know?" Generic Goon Student asks, right out of the blue.

Know what, I think. That Floy wrote *Handcrammin' Gorilla*? No, but—

"Like, yeah," Shrill Broad blurts out.

Even Fatties One and Two chime in.

"Why do you think we barely said much about it?"

"It's different to have a professor's work to read."

"Really, bro?"

"You'd know that if you read it…"

I start to wonder if they're really all saying these things, or if that's my head talking.

"Let me spell this out." Floy stands in the center of one of the aisles between our seats. "*Handcrafted Epyllia* is the story of two children, Soleas. Both are deaf. Despite this, their bond steadies them through thick and thin. When lip-reading isn't enough, their sign language is. When speech can't unite them, the language of their hand motions builds that bridge. That's the *hand* part of *Handcrafted*. It's something they create together. It's something they cherish."

The student with the phone keeps filming as a tear rolls down Mr. Floy's face, and I don't even have the scrap of an urge to call him a pussy.

"But then, in the epilogue, a day-drunk driver swerves through their neighborhood and runs one of the boys down, killing him on impact. And that's it. Abrupt, but finished. But what the story doesn't detail is how this took the other boy away from the world for a while, how it soundlessly tore him apart. He sat there, being forced to imagine what that crunch of bone-on-car sounded like. He was involuntarily detached from it because the volume in his little block of reality was too low. He couldn't even hear himself cry as he mourned this loss in the middle of the street, the dead boy's blood soaked into his shirt."

Generic Goon Student is frozen.

Shrill Broad and Fatties One and Two are frozen.

The chair-pounders, cat-callers, boo'ers, they're all frozen.

I'm frozen, too.

"I kept these parts out because they're more personal. Omitting them was the right thing to do. That decision was, however, supposed to lead to a better meaning by the end of the semester. You were all supposed to dissect the boys' relationship, trying to determine how the one remaining could find solace in any of it. This was supposed to take our class on an ultimately fulfilling journey, not this shit you've backed me into."

This breakdown is going to hit YouTube very, very hard, and now I'm sharing center stage with the Mr. Hyde side of Mr. Floy.

And now he's approaching me faster.

"What? Should I stop? Should I be fired for this?"

I backpedal. He advances.

"Well let me tell you something else, Soleas. Cochlear implants aren't all they're cracked up to be."

What, I ask.

Without hesitation, Mr. Floy pulls off what I realize is a wig. A convincing one, too. Hooking around his ear and attached to his bare scalp is an implant that the long, russet-shaded hair had been able to hide.

"I shouldn't hate this, but I do. I shouldn't be ashamed of it, but I hate the whole goddamn thing," he spits out, pointing heatedly at the device. "The internal bit, the processor, feel latched onto my head like niggling ticks. I shake myself awake at night, feeling phantom vibrations, thinking I taste metal and worrying about it breaking and rupturing into my skull.

"You don't know what this is like," he continues. "I can't roughhouse with my son, Isaiah. I hate the battery-changing. I hate feeling like I'm host to a metal slug I can't remove if I still want to hear. And I hate that I could've gotten one with a slimmer electrode, giving me a wider spectrum of sound, but I didn't because my family has been in an awful financial pinch for years, both my parents' generation and now, of course, mine."

Look, I say—

"But most of all, aside from the drama, I hate being told I can't do this, that and the other, and I abhor with this same panging ache having to inscribe this message into the fleshy, lightweight, unused, undeserving brains of implausibly shitty people like you."

The class, unmoving, looks like a snapshot into the eye of a storm.

"Hecklers are one thing. You're playing a game you don't belong in."

His face is now inches from mine, the smell of his anger wafting into me, his nostrils flaring.

"Oh, and not only is an epyllion, plural form epyllia, a shorter kind of an epic poem, but *Handcrafted Epyllia* is an anagram for *Deaf Children at Play*."

The hushed *oohs* that come out of the rest of the class say it all.

If verbal showdowns are a thing, then this is his victory.

I look at his cochlear implant. Then I look at the class, putting myself in their heads.

Damn, son, some of them probably think.

"Anything to say, Soleas?" Mr. Floy asks.

Talk about emasculated...another thinks, I'm sure.

He's just gonna take that?

Doesn't he have a comeback?

Here's a tip: don't get in others' heads. It leads to this.

"Too bad the driver didn't hit you, instead."

The next thing I know, his fists and the two cold, steel rings he's wearing hit my ear, then my jaw.

I topple into a daze before I hit the floor.

"Still blissful, are you?" he puffs out.

Not even a vowel escapes as I groan, my cheek pushed against the thin carpet.

Below everyone's feet, disoriented, the room spinning, one of my teeth lying next to my ear, Mr. Floy kneels over me, scowling.

"Now, get the fuck out of my class."

And I do.

The Big Top closes.

The curtain falls.

Game.

Set.

Match.

"Inscribing Soleas" was previously published in *Euphemism*.

A No That Became a (Very Long) Yes: Revisiting the Grunge in DFW's "Grunge American Novel"

Tony McMahon

> *What remains irreducible about this music [punk/grunge] is its desire to change the world. The desire is patent and simple, but it inscribes a story that is infinitely complex. The music came forth as a no that became a yes, then a no again, then again a yes: nothing is true except our conviction that the world we are asked to accept is false. If nothing was true, everything was possible.*
>
> —Greil Marcus

Marcus writes about punk and grunge in *Lipstick Traces*, inspiring thoughts of David Foster Wallace's work and the title of this paper, but is there anything else that is familiar to us as Wallace scholars? I would suggest that the words "infinitely" and "complex" should both have very special resonances.

It's probably useful to compare this quote to one by Wallace himself, because I think the similarities are quite striking:

"The best postmodern fiction wasn't just credible as art; it seemed downright socially useful in its capacity for what countercultural critics called 'a *critical negation* that would make it self-evident to everyone that the world is not as it seems'" (1997, 66, emphasis in original).

And the person Wallace is quoting here? None other than Marcus himself.

Introduction

On its release in 1996, *Infinite Jest*, the book that would come to be widely regarded as David Foster Wallace's magnum opus, was called by the *New York Times* "the grunge American novel" (Bruni). In his 2013 Wallace biography, *Every Love Story is a Ghost Story*, D.T. Max spends a couple of pages examining both the similarities and the differences between his subject and the grunge band Nirvana, as well as the musical genre of grunge more generally. Max then postulates that Wallace would have been annoyed by comparisons to a music and a scene that flew in the face of his "recovery theology" (223).

I intend to take as my point of respectful departure the problematic nature of this assumption of Max's, suggesting instead that grunge and its ancestor punk are both musical movements whose ontology is almost completely in line with Wallace's, promoting both positivity and recovery through engagement and a sense of community.

It's my contention that the *New York Times'* assessment was wholly correct, that *Infinite Jest* is in fact *the* grunge American novel and, as such, the text is overdue for serious critical examination within this framework. In order to begin this process, I intended to examine briefly work by the rock cultural critic Greil Marcus, the "delinquent critique" of the Situationist International, and a scholarly text by McKenzie Wark. All of these, I argue, are potentially illuminating avenues for further critical examination of Wallace's great novel.

Finally, I will argue that, when seen in relation to recent work about punk and grunge, Wallace's masterwork begins to live in a completely new and academically exhilarating manner.

Inherent in the idea of a no becoming a yes is movement from negativity to positivity, and I think this is something that can be ineluctably said of *Infinite Jest*, that this is what, in many serious ways, the novel is actually *about*. As just one small example of this, we need only recall Mario Incandenza's description of Ennett House as "people...getting less unhappy" (101).

To be sure, countering this, there's a lot of human misery depicted in the book, but the two main characters—Hal Incandenza and Don Gately—are both seen to move inexorably from the first emotional (perhaps even existential) position to the latter, Gately possibly a little more straightforwardly so than Hal.

Having said that, though, Dutch Wallace scholar Allard den Dulk, talking about Hal at the chronological end but opening chapter of *Infinite Jest*, has recently claimed that:

> We can perhaps conclude that there is nothing wrong with Hal, but that a change has taken place, from self-reflexive irony and cynicism to an openness, to the formation of a self—a change the rest of the novel illustrates the desirability of—and conclude that there is something wrong with the society that is horrified by him (2014, 130)

This moving from a position of great ontological pessimism to one of confidence is something that I've experienced in many ways myself. For me, the catalyst for this motion away from what I considered the misery of conventional value systems was punk. Just briefly, punk in 1976 spoke to me in terms that strongly suggested I need not accept meekly what was then to be my ultra lower working class fate of spending my life working in a factory.

I should take considerable trouble to point out here that there is, of course, nothing wrong with this kind of life, if that is the choice one makes. The alarming thing, for me, and something that continues to give me the howling fantods to this very day, was that it felt like I had absolutely no agency in the matter.

Punk gave me agency though. It told me I could start my own band, write a novel, go to university, perhaps even travel to The Sorbonne and Illinois

State University and have smart people listen to what I had to say. The sense of community I found with other punks facilitated a radical change in my outlook towards life. I saw others in the process of becoming Other and deduced that my own formation of a self could be anything I desired it to be. As such, I suggest to you today that punk is not unrelated to Wallace's use of AA as a facilitator of similar self-building in *Infinite Jest*.

In fact, I would further suggest that Wallace's portrayal of AA and punk are, in fact, very close relatives: refusals (noes) that become engagements (yeses) in potentially the most personal and profound of all possible ways.

1. Punk to Grunge to Wallace and Back Again

I've been talking a lot about punk, but *Infinite Jest* is the *grunge* American novel, right?

In the fledgling field of punk studies, we don't need to look very hard, or very far, to surmise that punk and grunge are intimately related. For the purposes of this essay, I'll be using the two terms to mean pretty much the exact same thing.

But how do we go about tying Wallace up in all this? There is evidence if we just look a little more closely at some of the scholarship. While I'm not aware of any direct examination of Wallace and punk/grunge, there are lots of little hints.

I'll talk shortly about punk's relatedness to continental philosophy, but for now I'll suggest that Wallace the punk was first born when Zadie Smith went some way toward establishing his connection to existentialism:

> How poor we are at tracing literary antecedents, how often we assume too much and miss obvious echoes. Lazily we gather writers by nations, decades and fashions; we imagine Wallace the only son of DeLillo and Pynchon. In fact, Wallace had catholic tastes, and it shouldn't surprise us to find...Sartre. (264)

The way I've edited that quote is a bit of a stretch, I know, but still, that Wallace was deeply interested in continental philosophy—existentialism in particular—is essentially what Smith is saying.

This thread of Wallace's connection to existentialism is then picked up, half a decade later, by both Ramal and den Dulk in their essays contained in Bolger & Korb's *Gesturing Toward Reality: David Foster Wallace and Philosophy*. In fact, den Dulk has gone so far as to publish, very recently, an entire book on the subject. His rationale:

> The affinity with existentialism lies in the attitude of engagement that the novels of Wallace, Eggers and Foer express...a literary execution of Sartre's notion of pure reflection (connecting themselves to the world we live in)...thereby establish[ing] what Wittgenstein and Camus describe as a community of meaning. (2015, 265)

In *Lipstick Traces*, Marcus adroitly explains that punk is very much a descendent of continental philosophy: a school of thought that Smith and den Dulk suggest plays an important role in Wallace's work. As such, we can posit a kind of psychogeographical map linking Wallace all the way back to Dada, then to surrealism, existentialism, situationism, punk and grunge. Not for nothing, but we can also have quite a bit of fun thinking about him in terms of stops along the way.

Just finally, for this section, it's probably worth noting that existentialism is a philosophy that, in a very similar manner to punk or grunge, often gets a very bad rap. Almost universally considered negative or nihilist, my contention is that both movements are actually quite the opposite.

As Marcus puts it: "[punk] wasn't nihilism...negation is always political: it assumes the existence of other people, calls them into being" (9).

2. We Need to Talk About Max

As I've already alluded to, D.T. Max spends some time in the biography examining Wallace and the grunge (so also punk) band Nirvana.

I should probably begin this section of my essay with the caveat that I think Max's book is a terrific though whirlwind work. And he does rather hit the nail on the head regarding Wallace and grunge with the following:

> There was a shared look between writer and singers too. The unwashed hair with bandana, unlaced work boots, and old plaid shirts that Wallace had been wearing since Arizona were also now practically a uniform for anyone who felt disenchanted with the post-Reagan American culture of buying and owning. (221)

I only really take issue with Max on the subject of grunge, notably the idea of grunge references irritating Wallace, and what I think is the mistaken, *perhaps* egregiously so, statement that grunge's "undemanding hopelessness flew in the face of his [Wallace's] recovery theology" (223)

I will argue in the next section that both grunge and punk are in fact the antithesis of "undemanding hopelessness" and that, rather than flying in the face of Wallace's [or anyone else's] recovery theology, these musical styles in fact provide healthy alternatives to paradigmatic restraints that are in themselves constricting and anxiety-producing.

Max says that:
> Both music [grunge] and novel [*Infinite Jest*] implied that communication had gotten harder and harder, hitting walls of isolation too high to scale, reducing us to diminished gestures, preferences, grunts. (221)

There are a number of problems in this statement, I think. Firstly, communication that has been reduced to grunts and diminished gestures is nonetheless still communication. I can attest from personal experience that finding a community of other grunters leads to an extraordinary sense of empowerment and, as Wallace might say, "feeling less alone inside." So, rather than the idea that grunge makes communication "harder and harder," I would argue rather that communication becomes simply more specialised, more unique and community-centred, "words to make disruption precious," as Marcus puts it, words that have the ring—true or not—that they are being spoken for the very first time, and words that, I surmise, became much more valuable as a result.

This is backed up by den Dulk's assertion that grunts—in this case, Hal's at the beginning slash end of *Infinite Jest*—in fact tell us more about those listening (or more to the point, *not* listening) than they do about the person uttering them.

> Perhaps the perceived 'primitivity' of Hal's self-expression symbolizes Hal's desire for a more 'sincere'—and therefore perceived by the committee members as a 'primitive,' outmoded—conception of the self. (2015, 43, FN79)

3. Punk and Grunge as Community

I stated in my introduction that grunge slash punk are both musical movements whose ontology is almost completely in line with Wallace's.

I make this claim because punk is, ultimately, all about community. I would cite again my own personal experiences mentioned earlier, but for those who might still approach this assertion with scepticism, punk scholar Michelle Liptrot states that:

> Participants are unified not only by punk music, but also by some basic values that underlie this music, notably its anti-establishment and non-conformist sentiments and, crucially, its DIY ethic. (227)

This is from an article published in the refereed journal *Punk & Post-Punk*, and it's reasonably obvious from the title that the author is concerned with the idea of community. In addition, the existence of refereed journals on a subject strongly suggest community to me also.

But back to Wallace the punk, an image I'm acutely aware some might have a hard time reconciling. It's at this point that I probably should proffer my favourite interpretation of the meaning of the word: and it's simply dancing to your own drumbeat. Something I think every reader would agree—particularly with *Infinite Jest*—Wallace had going on big time.

Then there's this anecdotal definition of punk that I especially like. It is a quote from Billy Joe Armstrong, lead singer of Green Day, and I think it illustrates succinctly that punk is actually opposite to the way that most people understand it, as three-chord thrash and a uniform of torn leather and moccasins:

> A guy walks up to me and asks, 'What's punk?' So I kick over a garbage can and say, 'That's punk!' So he kicks over a garbage can and says, 'That's punk?' And I say, 'No that's trendy!'

Thinking for yourself, in other words. Does this remind anyone of Wallace's idea—most famously illustrated in "This is Water"—of making an entirely conscious decision about what it is we pay attention to in this life, despite having been told that this has already been decided for us? There are many ways it can be described, but regardless of which one you choose, it's my firm conviction that Wallace's work stands as one of this idea's truly great exemplars.

Again, Griel Marcus:

> The mystery of spectral connections between people long separated by place and time, but somehow speaking the same language…words to make disruption precious…. A fantasy of resistance—which by its nature almost had to be a fantasy of collectivity, of solidarity.

4. Reinvigorating *Infinite Jest* Through Punk

It's probably not unfair to ask at this stage, does a novel such as *Infinite Jest* really need invigorating? Can a book that is over a thousand pages long ever be seen to lack in any way for new interpretations? These are good questions, but I think that the answer is yes, and the reason the answer is yes (or perhaps a no that becomes a yes) is that we can learn so much about both disciplines from melding punk and Wallace studies.

I'll very briefly outline two strategies for beginning this process:

4 A—Lipstick Traces on Wallace

Greil Marcus' amazing book, *Lipstick Traces*, mentioned earlier, is an interesting text in that almost its entire *raison d'etre*, over almost 500 pages, is connecting punk and situationism.

Interestingly, there's been some work recently on Wallace and situationism. It sort of subtly makes its way into the *Companion* via Burn (82), Quinn (95) and Evans (175). And Wallace scholars Bart Thornton and Bill Lattanzi have spoken extensively on the subject at various conferences.

I'm sure I'm not alone in regarding this as an extraordinarily exciting development. As such, it might be possible to view Marcus here as some kind of bridging text.

4 B—The Beach Beneath Boylston Street

My second proposal for rebooting the punked version of *Infinite Jest* involves not just looking more closely at situationism and how it might relate to Wallace, but doing so especially in light of its practice as proposed by Wark:

> Perhaps critical [and literary/Wallace] theory needs to chart another path through the aftermath of May '68, one that does not take one or other royal road back to philosophy.... There are turning points where the monuments of the critical theory cannon intersect with more interesting back alleys: take the streets named Lefebvre, not Lacan; Jorn, rather than Althusser; Debord, not Foucault... Our species-being is builders of worlds. Should we consent to inhabit this given one as our resting place, we're dead already. (159)

Conclusion: Unknown (Wallace) Pleasures

In *Joy Division*, Grant Gee's 2006 documentary about the Manchester post-punk group of the same name, Tony Wilson, one of punk's foremost father figures, says that: "Punk enabled you to say 'Fuck you,' but somehow it couldn't go any further. Sooner or later someone was going to want to say, 'I'm fucked,' and that was Joy Division." This was also a notion that Nirvana, big Joy Division fans, later adopted. In the end, perhaps the most grunge thing about the grunge American novel is that it continues the trend of these utterances. What makes Wallace's masterpiece stand alone, however, is that it expands considerably on this communication by going two steps further. *Infinite Jest* is, ultimately, a no that becomes a resounding yes by saying this: "I'm fucked, perhaps we all are. Here, in this crazy-long book, is what we all should do about it. Together."

References

Bolger, Robert K, & Korb, Scott. *Gesturing Toward Reality: David Foster Wallace and Philosophy.* New York: Bloomsbury, 2014. Pring.

Bruni, Frank. "The Grunge American Novel." *The New York Times*, March 24, 1996. Print.

den Dulk, Allard "Good Faith and Sincerity: Sartrean Virtues of Self-Becoming in David Foster Wallace's *Infinite Jest*," Eds. Bolger, Robert K, & Korb, Scott. *Gesturing Toward Reality: David Foster Wallace and Philosophy.* New York: Bloomsbury, 2014. 199-220. Print.

---. *Existential Engagement in Wallace, Eggers and Foer: A Philosophical Analysis of Contemporary American Literature.* New York: Bloomsbury Academic, 2015. Print.

Gee, Grant, Dir. *Joy Division.* UK: Hudson Productions, 2007.

Grossman, Perry. "Identity Crisis: The Dialectics of Rock, Punk and Grunge." *Berkeley Journal of Sociology*, vol. 41, Youth and Youth Culture (1996-1997), 1996. 19-40. Print.

Heylin, Clinton. *Babylon's Burning: From Punk to Grunge.* London: Viking, 2007. Print.

Liptrot, Michelle. "'Different People with Different Views but the Same Overall Goals:' Divisions and Unities Within the Contemporary British DIY Subcultural Movement." *Punk & Post Punk*, 2:3, 2013. 213-229. Print.

Marcus, Greil. *Lipstick Traces: A Secret History of the Twentieth Century.* London: Martin Secker & Warburg Limited, 1989. Print.

Max, D.T.. *Every Love Story is a Ghost Story: a Life of David Foster Wallace.* New York: Viking, 2012. Print.

Ramal, Randy. "Beyond Philosophy: David Foster Wallace on Literature, Wittgenstein, and the Dangers of Theorizing," Eds. Bolger, Robert K, & Korb, Scott, *Gesturing Toward Reality: David Foster Wallace and Philosophy.* New York: Bloomsbury, 2014. 177-198. Print.

Smith, Zadie. "*Brief Interviews with Hideous Men*: The Difficult Gifts of David Foster Wallace" *Changing My Mind.* London: Penguin, 2009. 257-300. Print.

Wallace, David Foster and Costello, Mark. *Signifying Rappers.* London: Penguin, 1990. Print.

Wallace, David Foster. *A Supposedly Fun Thing I'll Never Do Again.* London: Little, Brown and Company, 1997. Print.

---. "E Unibus Pluram." *A Supposedly Fun Thing I'll Never Do Again.* London: Little, Brown and Company, 1997. 21-82. Print.

---. *Infinite Jest.* London: Little, Brown and Company, 1996. Print.

---. "Westward the Course of Empire Takes its Way." *Girl With Curious Hair.*

New York: W. W. Norton & Company, 1989. 231-373. Print.

Wark, M.. *The Beach Beneath the Street: the Everyday Life and Glorious Times of the Situationist International.* London: Verso, 2011. Print.

Football's Season's Over: Notes on a Suicide
Ruben E. Rodriguez

Sometime in November

The soft padding of tennis shoes on concrete snaps Zero's head towards that direction. His ears vacillate, picking up signals from all over until he begins to growl at something I've yet to see. A rough-looking white guy slowly shuffles under the yellow streetlight, at which point Zero crescendos into a full bark attack. The guy smiles at Zero. There's just something about a twelve-pound dog that no one finds intimidating.

—It's okay, I say. He doesn't bite.

But the guy is already bending to pet him, reduced to baby talk and cooing as Zero's cropped tail is helicoptering with delight.

—Do you have a cigarette? The guy asks, flipping out a Zippo, lifting the lid up and down until it gives a healthy click each time.

—Sorry, I don't smoke, I say as Zero is back and clawing at my leg, begging to be picked up.

—Good. Never start. He laughs as he continues walking to the convenience store a block away.

What would he have said if I did offer him a cigarette? Would he have spat in my direction, glaring in disappointment while gratefully accepting? I don't understand people who are addicted to light narcotics but need to preach to *you* how terrible their vice is in some scheme for you to never pick up their bad habits. It's meant to be a warning but comes off more as a cry for pity. Don't do this, they say. I did this and look how much my life sucks now.

Zero is still doing his hourly round about the yard. The days are getting bluer, broken up with short spans of sunlight. He probably knows that he won't be seeing the grass until March, April if we're unlucky. The sound of tennis shoes on concrete resounds from the opposite direction now as the rough-looking white guy crinkles and shoves the cellophane into his pocket and digs out his prize. The Zippo flies open and the sparks carve out the features of his face as he lights up.

Zero's lost interest in him now. The lighter clicks shut, the cigarette burns as he exhales a long, euphoric trail of smoke, like he's breathing for the first time. He lifts up his prize as he passes me.

—For those too afraid to pull the trigger, he says.

And like the laziest magic act ever performed, he's gone in a puff of smoke.

January 2

—Tyler shot himself, says Facebook.

—Tyler who?

I have no idea who my friends are talking about in their status updates. I don't know what happened and I don't know which Tyler is receiving saccharine and uninspired obituaries that are assaulting my news feed.

Like ripples, the amount of people you affect with your death goes out in waves; the biggest flowing from the point of impact and subsequent smaller waves pushing out farther until they hit someone like me, who doesn't know or particularly care. Suicide just seems like an intentional stirring of waves, unintentionally hurting those around you, and thus people are prone to throw labels in an attempt to assess the situation that no one asked them to.

—Tyler. You know, *Tyler*. You grew up with him.

I'm still drawing blanks.

—You went to grade school with him. He was the high school quarterback, remember?

What I do remember is a young Tyler who in fourth or fifth grade came over to my house and watched Dragon Ball Z with me once after school, but that was a completely different era. His family moved, we stopped talking, and now he might as well be a stranger.

I come to find out he shot himself New Year's Eve. There must have been a logical and clear reason behind putting a gun to your temple...right?

—His girlfriend broke up with him, my mom calls to tell me.

> She's a bit of a gossip, my mother. It's not her fault, her social circle (which consists of suburban whites and townies) has shrunk since the divorce. She doesn't really talk to my father unless it's something over legal issues, and my brother rarely calls either, so it's up to me to discuss the news coming out of Peoria, including crime rates, the state of my former high school marching band, neighborhood gossip, and the occasional suicide. Y'know, mom stuff.

But then again, suicide rarely seems to have a clear and logical reason. Depression shouldn't be fatal, and until recently it always seemed like a shitty motive to take your own life. Most people have it in their head that depression is just you being sad, because that's what makes the most sense. When life gives you lemons, turn your frown upside down, there's always a silver lining. Except that's not how it works.

Didn't he know there were 3.6 billion other women out there?

> Apparently he wanted this particular fish

My brother texts me.

It always seems petty or stupid. Let's say you're the former high school quarterback of a failing football team from a relatively racist, hick town that no one can find on a map. I can think of a handful of reasons why anyone would want to kill themselves after going to Limestone, but taking a bullet over a girl? That just seems so…blasé. But that's why it's suicide. It's personal; it doesn't have to make sense to anyone else.

> It looks like they had a son, too.

—Unwed teen pregnancy? Throw in an affair or a drug addiction and you're a few steps away from an MTV reality drama.

> On New Year's no less. Pretty bold resolution.

I laugh.
—I'm glad we can joke about this.
Because it's good to laugh when nothing else makes sense.

December 27

At Jimmy's Pub in Peoria, people press against each other, cradling drinks and trying to talk above the person next to them. College boys wear tight, plaid shirts because they think it makes them look good (it doesn't). Despite the December air, college girls wear short skirts and caked makeup and uneven spray tans, all in an attempt to look better (it fails). Whenever I go to a bar, there's the same nagging feeling I get whenever I go to a church, like my time could be better spent elsewhere.

Drinks are cheap in Central Illinois. It's rare to go above $60 here just for yourself. The rich kids bred from Chicago suburbanites, who all happen to live on Bradley's Greek row, are foaming at the mouth when they see the menu, and you can practically see the dollar signs roll in the bartender's eyes.

One of these rich kids is pointing at me. His name is Mike or Mitch or something.

—What's your name? Mike's yelling over the speakers.

—Oliver, I yell back.

—No it's not, he says. You can see the effort in his face. The thought process and balance necessary to get the hang of this whole gravity situation that he just now noticed was there.

—Why do you want to know?

—Because I'm buying a round and I want to know everyone's name.

He's reached that level of drunkenness where his face begins to turn red and fold into itself to where I can't really tell if he's frustrated or incontinent. One of my friends tells me this is a guy who spends $300 of his parents' money every weekend.

—So you'll buy everyone a drink and I never have to talk to you again? I say.

—Sure, he says, not expecting or being particularly in the mood to play my games.

—Then you can call me Oliver.

—I'll just call you Jose, he amuses himself before disappearing.

A friend of mine, Zack, comes back with two $5 pints of Guinness. He is intelligent beyond his years with a receding hairline to match.

—It's poison really, he says setting the glasses down. People come together at the end of the long week and pay too much money to poison themselves to unwind or deal with the thought of next week. He takes a small gulp from each of his Guinnesses. There's a thesis somewhere in there, he says.

Zack can understand this; he was a slight alcoholic less than a year ago. He's been an avid drinker since he was a freshman in high school. He once told me that he hit rock bottom when realizing how he couldn't function without a drink. He would just sit in the dark and weep.

—Every weekend people show up in droves and hand over money to a man who offers to kill their liver just a little bit.

I tell him I like the idea enough to steal it. The image of a casual Kevorkian sitting behind a bar, handing out small doses of relief until problems melt away; shots to those who want their problems to go away a bit faster. Assisted until brain dead, they come with friends because they don't want to die alone.

Mike or Mitch or something comes back with a tray full of shots and hands a glass to everyone.

—Here you go, Cuervo. He hands over a glass and I smell cinnamon. Of course it's Fireball.

Mitch raises his shot and he's trying to gather his thoughts to make a passable toast or something to draw the attention to him. I'm already bored, and just wanting to piss him off, I slosh my drink down and slam the shot glass back on the table, making sure to connect with Mike's eyes and his stupid, annoyed, drunk face. I smirk and go back to talking with Zack before realizing how much of an ass I was to this complete stranger and how lonely he may actually be.

January 3

What do you call someone who commits suicide?

—A coward, is Tom's immediate response. Tom grew up with Tyler, too. We both knew him; both had him over for birthday parties, boxcar racing, and soccer games. I didn't want Tom to elaborate, because I'm already pretty well versed in the Tao of Tom.

—Selfish? Stephanie isn't sure what to call them. I'm sure he had his reasons, she says. Nothing's clear as day, everyone's a bit fucked up.

—What do you call someone who commits suicide? I text my brother.

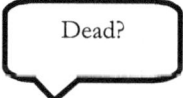

Dead?

—That's not really the answer I'm looking for.

If there is an opinion I trust more than any other about the fucked-upness of the world, it is Stephanie's. Her life is dramatic. Like, HBO dramatic. Stephanie has managed to live through boyfriends who were too neurotic, boyfriends who were too "nice", boyfriends who weren't too keen on sobriety, being kicked out of her house, homelessness, major deaths in the family, finding out that that the man she lived with and called 'Dad' was not her biological father, while her real dad lives a few blocks away but is a meth addicted hobo along with other various forms of bullshit within the last eight years. All of which has managed to make Stephanie the most well-adjusted, optimistic, and most genuine person I've ever met.

Tom's views on life are pretty simple and full of innocence; it's the perfect antidote to my cynicism, which is probably why we've been friends for over twenty years. A well-rounded, mechanical engineer, Tom's a rare breed. Deeply set within the machinations of a mechanical engineer's brain, there must be a slot marked HUMAN COMPASSION with a missing hard drive. Instead, there must be a large chunk marked GENERAL LACK OF EMPATHY AND INABILITY TO PROCESS NONVERBAL COMMUNICATION. AND METAPHORS. YOU JUST CAN'T UNDERSTAND METAPHORS. How Tom has managed to escape the stereotypical engineer mindset to become a well-rounded and thoughtful human being is beyond me.

If you wanted an answer you should have Googled it. You text me, you get sass.

—Cheeky son of a bitch.

> She's your mother, too.

My dad only looks up from the newspaper when I tell him that the kid who was in Cub Scouts with me killed himself.

—Oh…that was dumb of him…he flips a page.

Maybe I set my expectations too high. I finally follow my brother's advice and straight up Google *suicide*. So what do you call someone who commits suicide? Suicide. The person is the action is the event. Mystery solved. End of story. The results don't satisfy me. People trying to comprehend the actions of others lead to hypotheses that just make the most sense for themselves. They'll make up their own reasons; they'll call them sick, or sad, or stupid, or not thinking clearly, or use some other demeaning or melancholy definition. Of course outsiders aren't going to understand it; they're not the demographic.

When Hemingway was depressed, with too much iron in his blood and his mind fried by electroconvulsive therapy, did he see the shotgun as selfish? The Hemingways, post-World War II, led a troubling life after a plane crash in Africa left Ernest with a skull fracture that wasn't immediately treated. He wasn't the same after that. It wasn't until Ernest and Mary were in Italy that he finally received the appropriate medical attention, months after the incident.

A fan of alcohol, Hemingway eventually relied on drinking to dull the pain (which was frequent). Who needs brain functionality when you're actively trying to push away the thought that a few teaspoons of your cerebral fluid was left somewhere between Entebbe and Venice?

The accident combined with alcohol left him unable to collect his thoughts. He stopped writing. Combine that with fits of depression, illnesses, paranoia fueled by the FBI, and several trips to the Mayo Clinic for ECT sessions, until finally diagnosed with the fatal hemochromatosis (in which patients are subjected to bloodletting as treatment), and the gun cabinet in the basement storeroom is becoming more reasonable.

The question everyone seems to be asking themselves when they think about Hemingway loading the rounds into the shotgun is why he did it. The reasoning behind Hemingway's death is easy to answer for most people because they could just as easily pick a motive out of a hat and come up with their own answer that they find suitable. Will the contestant choose: alcoholism, brain damage, FBI conspiracy theories, depression, disease, or a stunted creative output? They either don't understand or don't want to understand, so they'll package it into a category easily swallowed. Whatever the reason, the conclusion everyone reaches is unanimous: the shotgun provided a way out. A vanishing act, a trap door, an exit for when the show's over. Hemingway, seeing few options between dying now or living a pain-ridden life and *then* dying, chose his own terms on how he was going to go out. And in true Hemingway fashion, he didn't even leave a note.

So what do you call someone who commits suicide?

Coward?

Selfish?

Dumb?

Or an escape artist?

Author Here, IYI: Preformance of Author/Text/Reader Relationships in the Margins of DFW's Works[1]

Nathan Seppelt

> *There's another level that a piece of fiction is a conversation. There's a relationship set up between the reader and the writer that's very strange and very complicated and hard to talk about.*[2]
> *So what, we're going to pretend, we're going to pretend that we're sitting in the same room?*[3]

Presenter here.[4] Although that probably goes without saying. You can see me; I can see you. The only thing between us is this podium and a couple metres of empty space. You'll hear what I'm saying as I say it, where I say it, and if that's not enough you can grab me by the lapels and look into my face and figure out just exactly what one single thing I mean.[5]

So here I am. Nathan Seppelt, Independent Scholar from Adelaide, Australia. The paper I'm talking about today is *Author Here, IYI*[6] and is basically about the ways Wallace uses marginalia—including footnotes, endnotes, prefaces and forewords, *Host*'s boxed notes, and even headings—to explore and perform some key questions about author/text/reader relationships.

But what if I wasn't talking to you here today? What if we were communicating through a written text, especially one we understand as being fictional?[7] What if I was armed with a shit-ton of philosophy and lit-theory about the death of the author, iterability of writing, artifice of text, author vs. persona, Derrida, Barthes, etcetera etcetera?[8]

Would that give me the tools and make it easier for me to communicate meaningfully and directly with you, or complicate it?

What if I've been writing and reading postmodern literature that repeatedly, hollowly exposes the artifice of text and persona as written, but doesn't say: yes, but when you peel back the artifice here's what's real, here's *who's* real, and really trying to communicate with you. And I've become so frustrated with this kind of writing that I've reached a personal crisis, of sorts.

I'm not actually talking about myself any more: I'm talking about David Foster Wallace. When Wallace wrote his *Westward*,[9] he was at his most frustrated with texts that pointed out 'this text is written', but by pushing this idea to its most extreme and, really, trying to exhaust it,[10] he found that on the other side of 'this text is written' is the question 'by whom?'

I would argue that throughout the rest of his writing, beyond *Westward*, Wallace would strive to explore this very question. In doing so, and being the theory slash philosophy junkie that he was, Wallace takes a couple of prevalent assumptions about the nature of authors and the relationships they have with their texts and explores them through a range of performances.

Today I'll focus on these two assumptions:

One: Either the author is responsible for, or determines, their text's meaning; or the reader is, via their (the reader's) interpretation of it. Wallace discusses this directly in a number of nonfiction pieces including *Joseph Frank's Dostoevsky*,[11] *Greatly Exaggerated*[12] especially, and even in some fiction—like "Pop Quiz 9" in *Octet*, where he compares an author to a dramatist "coming onstage from the wings and reminding you that what's going on is artificial and that the artificer is him (the dramatist)."[13]

Assumption two: That either the author is absent from/external to the text or is present/expressed within the text. This one relates to the iterability of the text and the absence of author this requires and signifies—so is pretty much on the Derrida side of the "death of the author" fence. Again, Wallace discusses this and Derrida most overtly in *Greatly Exaggerated*: the thing I said earlier about lapels and grabbing was paraphrased from an especially good paragraph about this.[14]

You're probably way ahead of me already and noticed that the two assumptions I've chosen to focus on I've presented as binary oppositions: either the author is responsible for the text's meaning or they're not. Either the author is present or absent; they're either within the text or outside it.

So, besides the whole good-old 'getting to the centre of meaning by looking to the margins' type thing[15] Derrida so mindbendingly exemplifies in his *Margins of Philosophy*,[16] there's another really good reason marginalia is useful to Wallace and our reading of him here: marginalia, especially in Wallace's hands, themselves defy these binary oppositions.

Marginalia is simultaneously both part of the text and outside of it: it comes from the same source as the main text and occupies the same space—we can even say that it is contained in the same artefact. But at the same time marginalia distances and excludes itself from the main text by commenting,[17] criticising,[18] qualifying,[19] or clarifying[20] the main text. Nadel says that marginalia exhibits "the double consciousness of the text."[21]

This special status becomes a powerful tool for Wallace as he uses marginalia to restructure his texts: what would otherwise be situated inside the main text is brought outside and vice versa. His footnotes constantly do this in small ways,[22] but Wallace also does this on a much larger scale—particularly when he's exploring the relationships between authors, readers and the text between them. A few examples:

"Pop Quiz Nine" in *Octet* actually, overtly focuses on the relationships between author, reader and the text that comes between them.[23] Being #9 in a series that *should* contain eight Pop Quizzes this PQ appears to be written 'outside' the 'Octet,' but the fact that there are only actually three-and-a-halfish other PQs before this one[24] places PQ9 somewhere between the fourth and fifth actual piece in the cycle, moving this discussion on author and relationships from outside the Octet—literally—to its very centre.[25]

A little less subtly, the "THE END" that appears at the end of the single footnote to *Good Old Neon*[26] does the opposite, placing the main text after the occurrence of the footnote—including the introduction of the character David Wallace, whose name matches the author's—beyond or outside the close of the story.

Endnote 78 in *Infinite Jest*[27] has a similar effect on the book's first chapter. The note indicates that as of 15 December Y.D.A.U. —presumably the time of writing—the Year of Glad sponsorship is still pending approval.

But: *IJ*'s drum-tight first chapter is clearly set in Year of Glad. These are the first three words of the book.[28] The endnote moves Hal's first chapter beyond the whole apparatus of main text and footnotes, to outside everything else that's going on between the main text's and endnote's authors[29] and reframes the opening chapter's two big "metafictional titty-pincher"'s:[30] "I am in here"[31] and the casually tossed-out "holographically mimetic."[32] It's important to note too that at the same time this restructuring also entails an inwards, centre-directed movement by the endnotes.

The most obvious example, though, is *The Pale King*'s "Author's Foreword."

The named Author, David Wallace, uses the foreword to address the reader directly and explicitly spell out that what we're reading is nonfiction,[33] that it will look like fiction,[34] and why.[35] He talks about a book's normal "unspoken contract"[36] between author and reader, the terms of which contract "always depend on certain codes and gestures that the author deploys in order to signal the reader what kind of book it is, i.e., whether it's made up vs. true,"[37] and why that's actually misleading in this case.

The sticky point is that all this is not laid out right at the start of the book as expected, but has been moved, at the publisher's insistence,[38] 63 pages[39] into the main text. This restructuring means that all the codes and gestures for fiction have already been deployed and all this Foreworded explication is actually read under the contract that it's fictional.

Wallace is more or less asking us readers to make a decision here: to disregard the implicit author/reader contract that's coded throughout all the text we've read so far and accept what he says he means, and enter into the author/reader contract for *non*fiction; or whether it's the text's own pre-existing operation to set up the "unspoken" contract for fiction that's more important.

* * *

Now, the other thing that's disproportionately interesting (and important) for the amount of time I've left for it[40] is the way Wallace uses marginalia to fracture and pluralise the author's/narrator's identity.

On a fairly fundamental level, he does this between the 'real' author and the manifestation or expression of that person within their text. The "Author's Foreword" in *The Pale King* is, again, an obvious and valuable example.

The foreword begins with "Author here. Meaning the living human being holding the pencil."[41] The way Wallace uses the word "here"[42] in this passage situates the author with the reader, through the text. Because the author is not obviously immediately[43] present with the reader, his presence is mediated through the text; he can be said to be present in the text.

But then Wallace complicates it by very specifically situating himself outside or behind the text. He writes, "addressing[44] you from my Form 8829-deductible home office at 725 Indian Hill Blvd., Claremont 91711 CA, on this fifth day of spring, 2005."[45] By providing both the specific address and the time of his writing, Wallace is bringing himself back out of the text. And by specifying the date in particular, his "I'm here" includes the disclaimer "but only on March 24, 2005." Which is to say he's not really here.[46]

By asserting right from the "Author's Foreword"'s first sentence that he, the author, *is* here and then proving that he is somewhere not-here, Wallace forces the reader to consider both situations as simultaneously possible—replacing the either/or proposition of our second assumption with both/and.

Even the most unambiguous-seeming datum about the author provided in the foreword is in fact fraught with ambiguity and signifies identities around the author that multiply and converge. As we later learn, Wallace's social security number originally signified *The Pale King*'s other David F. Wallace, with whom the author's persona has a complicated ontological relationship.[47]

The performances in *Infinite Jest* are way more complicated[48] and where a lot of the real fun is. *Infinite Jest* is presented as a text that reports rather than one that is constructed.[49] A big part of this is the way the authors are presented as people who have assembled the text from within the world in which it takes place.[50] These authors' identities are complexly fractured[51]—mostly thanks to the endnotes—and their identities are unknown. The endnotes raise possibilities for the authors' identities and hints at which characters they may be.

I'm going to really disappoint you and not get into who the candidates are and why,[52] but what's noteworthy[53] here is that the text's clues point inwards, within the text. In *Infinite Jest*, Wallace so thoroughly situates the authors within the text that he almost completely absents[54] himself: the external, "real human" author. There's little we know for sure about *Infinite Jest*'s intra-textual authors' identities, but what we do know is that it is not someone completely external to the text: it is not Wallace.[55] All of this is not to say that there are no tensions between authors and narrators/personae at play in *Infinite Jest*[56]: they've just been transposed to a level where all parties are equal within the text and so are all equally, and simultaneously possible.

This (very brief) conclusion is probably a little late in the game to introduce something new, but it is something I've hinted at a couple of times already. One more binary opposition Wallace keeps in play with regard to everything I've spoken about so far: decidability vs. undecidability.

By showing that both poles of the binary oppositions Wallace explores are simultaneously possible, but conflict in complex and interesting ways, he shows that they are undecidable within (or from behind) the text. In his exploration of this binary—which ultimately is about the ability to decide—Wallace pushes it to the same question he asks of the idea that a text is written in the first place: "*by whom?*"[57]

Works Cited

Barthes, R 1977 *Image, Music, Text* trans. S Heath, Hill and Wang, New York.
Derrida, J 1978 *Writing and Difference*, trans. A Bass, U Chicago P, Chicago.
Derrida, J 1981 *Dissemination*, trans. B Johnson, TU Chicago P, Chicago.
Derrida, J 1982 *Margins of Philosophy*, trans. A Bass, U Chicago P, Chicago.
Derrida, J 1994 *Of Grammatology*, trans. GC Spivak, Motilal Banardass Publishers, Delhi.
Luther, C 2010 'David Foster Wallace: Westward with Jameson' in D Hering (ed.) *Consider David Foster Wallace: Critical Essays*, Sideshow Media Group P, Los Angeles, pp.49-61.
Max, DT 2012, *Every Love Story is a Ghost Story: A Life of David Foster Wallace* Granta P, London.
Miller, L 2012, 'Something Real American' in *David Foster Wallace: The Last Interview and Other Conversations*, Melville House P, Brooklyn, NY, pp.5-16.
Nadel, I 2012, 'Consider the Footnote' in S Cohen & L Konstantinou (eds.) *The Legacy of David Foster Wallace*, U of Iowa P, Iowa, pp.218-240.
Scocca, T 2012 'There Can Be No Spokesman' in *David Foster Wallace: The Last Interview and Other Conversations*, Melville House P, Brooklyn, NY, pp.19-51.
Wallace, DF 1989 'Westward the Course of Empire Takes its Way' in *Girl with Curious Hair*, W.W. Norton & Company, Inc., New York, NY, pp.231-373.
Wallace, DF 1996, *Infinite Jest*, Little, Brown & Company, New York, NY.
Wallace, DF 1997, *A Supposedly Fun Thing I'll Never Do Again*, Back Bay Books, New York, NY.
Wallace, DF 2001, 'Octet' in *Brief Interviews with Hideous Men*, Abacus, London, pp.111-136
Wallace, DF 2004, *Everything and More: A Compact History of Infinity*, W.W. Norton & Company, New York, NY.
Wallace, DF 2005a, *Consider the Lobster and Other Essays*, Abacus, London.
Wallace, DF 2005b *Oblivion*, Back Bay Books, New York, NY.
Wallace, DF 2011, *The Pale King*, ed. M Pietsch, Little, Brown & Company, New York, NY.
Wallace, DF 2012 *Both Flesh and Not: Essays*, Little, Brown &Company, New York, NY.
Wallace, DF & Costello M 2013, *Signifying Rappers*, Back Bay Books, New York, NY.

---

[1] Transcript of presentation of the same name.

[2] *Something Real American*, interview with Wallace as included in *David Foster Wallace: The Last Interview and Other Conversations* (Miller 2012 pp.11-2).

[3] Or a much cooler epigraph: Wallace talking to Tom Scocca (*There Can Be No Spokesman*) in the same collection of interviews as the first epigraph above (Scocca 2012 p.20).

[4] (Fell C, Bloomington-Normal Marriott Hotel & Conference Center. 1420 29 May, 2015.)

[5] Paraphrased (badly) from *Greatly Exaggerated* in *A Supposedly Fun Thing I'll Never Do Again* (Wallace 1997 p.140)

[6] For our current purposes, this 'transcript' is that paper.

[7] That this text is a transcript is essentially a fiction. I wrote these words at a desk in a room, on my own, and well ahead of the date specified in FN2; but I wholeheartedly recommend not going there.

[8] Again, *Greatly Exaggerated* (Wallace 1997 pp.138-45) is a good starting point. *Every Love Story is a Ghost Story: A Life of David Foster Wallace* (Max 2012 pp. like 38, 56, & 57's "Wallace tried to make friends with them in his usual way by asking how they could call themselves fiction writers without having read Derrida") has some points of interest, too.

[9] (*Westward the Course of Empire Takes its Way* (Wallace 1989 pp.231-373))

[10] Re this and the uncomfortably unfootnoted previous paragraph, see *David Foster Wallace: Westward with Fredric Jameson* (Luther 2010 p.49).

[11] eg. its seventh footnote (Wallace 2005a p.259).

[12] eg. "…to appreciate why the metaphysical viability of the author is a big deal you have to recognize the difference between a writer—the person whose choices and actions account for a text's features—and an author—the entity whose intentions are taken to be responsible for a text's meaning." (Wallace 1997 p.139) —and that's just the beginning.

[13] (Wallace 2001 p.125)

[14] The paragraph's climax: "For Barthes, Derrida, and Foucault, writing is a better animal than speech because it is iterable; it is iterable because it is abstract; and it is abstract because it is a function not of presence but of absence: the reader's absent when the writer's writing, and the writer's absent when the reader's reading." (Wallace 1997 p.140). There's also some great stuff in *The Empty Plenum* eg. "the truth of 'I write' yields only the existence of text." (Wallace 2012 p.84) and so on.

[15] The fact that footnotes can be used to define or clarify the meaning of terms in the main text (eg. FNs16-18, ch.2A in *Signifying Rappers* (Wallace & Costello 2013 p.47) is an easy and low-level example. The simultaneous climax of several different narrative threads in *Federer Both Flesh and Not* in its final footnote is a much more satisfying example (Wallace 2012 p.32).

[16] (Derrida 1982)

[17] eg. *Octet*'s PQ9's FN7 (Wallace 2001 p.131)

[18] "I know I'm not putting this well; it seems too complicated to be put well." (Wallace 1997 p.171)

[19] eg. most of the first 15 or so footnotes to *Tennis Player Michael Joyce's Professional Artistry as a Paradigm of Certain Stuff About Choice, Freedom, Limitation, Joy, Grotesquerie, and Human Completeness* (Wallace 1997 pp.213-22). For the especially paranoid close reader, Wallace seems to be playing a game: these early footnotes qualify portions of the essay's main text that are about Joyce & the process for qualifying for a tennis tournament. As a kind of vindication for the paranoid close reader, the term "meta-Qualies" appears in FN9 (Wallace 1997 p.219).

[20] eg. *Everything and More*'s FN22, ch.2b (Wallace 2004 p.66)

[21] (Nadel 2012 p.219)

[22] It's often stuff like *A Supposedly Fun Thing*'s footnoted "about whom if there's any

editorial justice you'll learn a lot more *someplace below.*" (Wallace 1997 p.293: emphasis mine).

[23] eg. "…part of what you want these little Pop Quizzes to do is to break the textual fourth wall and kind of address (or 'interrogate') the reader directly" (Wallace 2001 pp.124-5): But seriously, pretty much the whole of PQ9.

[24] PQs 4, the "abortive" 6 (Wallace 2001 p.120), 7, and 6A. Plus "the now-quartet's" and its attached FN4: "(or rather duo-plus-dual-attempts-at-the-third,' whatever the Latinate quantifier for this would be)" (Wallace 2001 p.129).

[25] I could probably convince you much more easily if I were right there with you and could write out a number line 1-9 on a cocktail napkin or something, draw one box around all the numbers 1-8, circle the 9, and draw an arrow from the 9 to the space right between the 4 and the 5.

[26] (Wallace 2005b p.179)

[27] (Wallace 1996 p.999)

[28] (Wallace 1996 p.3, obviously)

[29] EN25 "More like July-October, actually.'"s ", actually." (Wallace 1996 p.994) is an early sign of diffraction/disagreement between the book's intra-textual authors.

[30] (Wallace 2011 p.67)

[31] (Wallace 1996 p.3). The important thing being the shift in what exactly "here" is referring to.

[32] (Wallace 1996 p.7). Ignoring Hal's opinion on Denis Gabor (p.12), that *The New Shorter OED* (1993) defines holograph as "A document etc. wholly written by hand by the person named as its author." warrants some consideration.

[33] "All of this is true. This book is really true.", "what follows is, in reality, not fiction at all" (both Wallace 2011 p.67, plus there's more).

[34] (Wallace 2011 p.72 from "The point I'm trying to drive home here" onwards.)

[35] *Ibid.* See also FN37 below.

[36] (Wallace 2011 p.73)

[37] *Ibid.*

[38] Quick aside (some of which has actually been moved here from the original presentation): The role that editors and publishers have in influencing an author's text—especially what's included vs. what isn't—and the possibilities for its meaning and even the author's persona is a recurring theme in Wallace's footnotes. Besides *The Pale King* here, or those like the one mentioned in FN21 above, gems like the "Optional Foreword" to *Up Simba* (Wallace 2007 pp.156-9) and Wallace's "I don't think there was really any persona there at all, except what emerged through the fact the thing was getting cut over and over again" and what follows it (Scocca 2012 p.47) are definitely worth a read.

[39] Curiously, the foreword's second footnote claims it (the foreword) has been moved 79 pages into the text (Wallace 2011 p.67 (NB: the first page of text is p.3. Even accounting for the "Editor's Note", title and copyright pages etc. doesn't account for the anomaly)).

[40] (Given that this is a transcript of a 15 min. presentation.)

[41] (Wallace 2011 p.66)

[42] Which, by the way, he does in footnotes all over the place. Case in point: the first footnote of *Everything and More* (which is all about IDing the author) includes the

words "Your author here" (Wallace 2004 p.2).

[43] (corporeally)

[44] This double entendre on "address" just blows my mind: by juxtaposing the author's text as an "address" against a real world location, he kinda situates himself in *both*.

[45] (Wallace 2011 pp.66-7)

[46] Because Derrida. "The absence of the sender, the addressor, from the marks that he abandons, which are cut off from him and continue to produce effects beyond his presence and beyond the present actuality of his meaning, that is, beyond his life itself, this absence, which however belongs to the structure of all writing" (Derrida 1982 p.313).

[47] (ultimately due to a systematic "failure to distinguish between two different internal David Wallaces" (Wallace 2011 p.308).)

[48] Like, trying to decoct Pemulis's and Hal's statuses as authors of the text in endnote 123 (Wallace 1996 pp.1023-5) (but also their relationships to the EN itself, seeing as it's just *plonked* there without any heading or title or anything (not to mention that the endnote also exposes Hal as the main text author around page 322. Or that Hal (or Pemulis?) has inserted a P.S. into EN127 (Wallace 1996 p.1025), which endnote doesn't seem to be written by either of them). Or there's Himself's status as *Auteur* vs. the role of narrators in at least a dozen of his films, according to the EN24 filmography (Wallace 1996 pp.985-93). Or even the author's uncertainty about what has been said in the text and by whom: EN94: "It's surely been spelled out already" (Wallace 1996 p.1003).

[49] cf. Marlon Bain: "It is not that I think Orin Incandenza is a liar, but that I think he has come to regard the truth as *constructed* instead of *reported*." (emphasis original); which cf. Hal: "'You of all people, O. You know that [deconstructed] was the one word [Himself] hated more than—'" in conjunction with James Incandenza's own: "… they assumed the babble(/babel) was some self-conscious viewer-hostile heavy-art directorial pose, instead of [Incandenza's films'] radical realism." (Wallace 1996 pp.1048, 251 & 836 respectively).

[50] There are plenty of clues scattered throughout *IJ*'s endnotes, like references to "Subsidized Time" (eg. ENs 43, 62, 78) or citations of "in-world" references (eg. EN64) (all these Wallace 1996 995, 996, 999, & 997 respectively).

[51] eg. see FNs 28 and 47 above.

[52] (but if you do want to play that game, comparing Bain's wordy, footnoted letter to Steeply (Wallace 1996 pp.1047-52) against the novel as a whole could be an interesting place to start…)

[53] Pun *really* not intended.

[54] Another way the "author" absents themself from the endnotes is by avoiding referring to themselves using personal pronouns. ENs 117 and 119 are the best examples of this (Wallace 1996 p.1022). EN278's "Where was *Mrs*. Pemulis all this time […] is what I'd want to know." (Wallace 1996 p.1052) makes this absence conspicuous.

[55] There's something uncomfortably odd about experiencing all of *Infinite Jest* and then seeing, on what is effectively p.1081, "ABOUT THE AUTHOR" all in caps w/ one paragraph of Wallace's bio; at least if you have the same edition of *IJ* I have.

[56] eg. see FN28 above.

[57] See *Octet*'s final sentence (Wallace 2001, p.136).

Author Biographies

Corrie Baldauf is an Assistant Professor of Art at Eastern Michigan University. Her art practice is based out of a shared studio space in Corktown, Detroit. Baldauf's research has appeared in *German Art Magazine*, *Magazine for Contemporary Drawing*, *Lufthansa Exclusive Magazine*, and *Hyperallergic*. Her artwork has been internationally exhibited and is included in major collections such as Daimler Financial Services, Farmington Hills, Michigan; Nerman Museum of Contemporary Art and Sprint Corporation, Overland Park, Kansas. Twitter: @CorrieBaldaufWebsite: corriebaldauf.com.

Jeffrey Calzaloia is a novelist whose ambitious work may not achieve commercial success but whose investment in producing high-quality literary fiction remains strong. Inspired by novelists such as John Crowley, Toni Morrison, Gene Wolfe, Cormac McCarthy, Junot Díaz, Samuel R. Delany, Marcel Proust, and (of course) David Foster Wallace, as well as poets such as Gerard Manley Hopkins, Wallace Stevens, Leonie Adams, and John Brooks Wheelwright, Calzaloia is a fresh young talent to watch out for in the years to come.

Jane L. Carman is a former Sutherland Fellow, founder of the David Foster Wallace Conference, and PhD reciepient at Illinois State University. She is founder of the reading series Festival of Language and a reading eXperiment, as well as Lit Fest Press and *Festival Writer*. Her book, *Tangled in Motion*, was published by Journal of Experimental Fiction Books in 2015. Other creative and critical work can be found in *elimae*, *580-Split*, *American Book Review*, *Devil's Lake*, *Palooka*, *Blue Collar Review*, *JAC*, *Santa Clara Review*, and others.

A writer and documentary filmmaker, **Jodie Childers** wrote and produced the documentary, *The Other Parade*, and she is currently codirecting a film about Pete Seeger's environmental legacy. Her creative writing has been published in *Feral Feminisms*, *Eleven Eleven*, *Poetry East*, the *Portland Review*, and other literary journals. She received an MFA from Brooklyn College, and she is currently pursuing a PhD in English with a concentration in American studies at the University of Massachusetts, Amherst.

Amy L. Eggert teaches composition, literature, and creative writing for Bradley University in Peoria, Illinois. She has a PhD in English Studies from Illinois State University with a specialization in trauma theory and creative writing. She is the author of *Scattershot: Collected Fictions* (2015) from Lit Fest Press, and her work appears in several literary journals, *Festival Writer*, *Bluffs Literary Magazine*, and the *American Book Review*.

Usama Ehsan received his BA in English with a concentration in Literary Theory at UC Irvine and his MA in English at California State University of Fullerton. He has also studied Deutsch Philology, Philosophy, and English Philology at Freie University of Berlin in Germany. Part of his Master's thesis, "Identity Beyond Consumer Ethos in David Foster Wallace's *The Pale King*," was presented at the Second Annual David Foster Wallace Conference.

Danielle S. Ely completed her Master's Thesis about *Infinite Jest*, titled "Into the Womb of Solipsism: The Entertainment as 'Speculum,'" in 2011. She has presented instantiations of her thesis at conferences like Sex…or Something Like It, Multiplicities: Mapping Identity Through Literature in Madrid, and the David Foster Wallace Conference. Her complete thesis is available on Proquest. Her work can also be found in Lit Fest Press's *Normal 2014*. She is an adjunct instructor of English at Columbia-Greene Community College, Hudson Valley Community College, and Dutchess County Community College.

Rich Hanson is a Supervisor Consumer Safety Inspector at a packing plant in Monmouth, Illinois, where he resides with his wife, Nancy. "Dreams Are Slaughtered Here Too" is a selection from a number of packing house stories that he hopes to publish after he retires and it is prudent to do so. Rich graduated from the University of Minnesota–Duluth with a major in English and a minor in food science from Mississippi State University.

Eric Izant is an English PhD candidate at the University of Colorado at Boulder. He is in the midst of writing his dissertation, which explores the relationship between drugs and language in contemporary literary works by William S. Burroughs, Terence McKenna, Thomas Pynchon, and David Foster Wallace. He also teaches modern and contemporary literature classes at CU Boulder and for the past three semesters has had the pleasure of teaching a course centered on *Infinite Jest*. Going forward, Izant hopes to obtain his PhD and continue teaching at a university level.

Jeff Jarot is a writer who teaches high school English in Plainfield, Illinois. He holds a BA in English from Illinois Wesleyan University, a BA in English Education and MA in English from Illinois State University, and an MA in English from Northern Illinois University. Jarot's short story "Home Movies" and an excerpt from his novella *Zuzu's Petals* (Lit Fest Press, 2016). His previous Wallace scholarship was also featured in *Normal 2014*.

Carissa Kampmeier earned a Master's degree in English Studies from Illinois State University. Her research interests include the ways that contemporary American fiction is both reacting to and influenced by the postmodern movement, the genre of the mixtape as a form of life-writing, and the critical analysis of horror films.

Ashlie M. Kontos is a master's student of English at the University of Texas at Tyler. Her research interests include shame; literary theory—specifically metamodernism; post-Holocaust Jewish literature; and the literature and philosophy of David Foster Wallace. She has her BA in English with minors in history and classical studies. Her essay "Nomina Nuda Tenemus: Jonathan Safran Foer Finding Meaning Within Empty Names, or (re)Construction of Deconstruction" won the University of Louisiana at Lafayette's Darrell Borque Award (2012) and was published in *Media, Technology, and Imagination* in 2013 by Cambridge Scholars Publishing. Her essay "'It takes great personal courage to let yourself appear weak': DFW on Shame, Addiction and Healing" appeared in *Normal 2014*, which she co-edited in 2015.

Dave Laird is a high school humanities teacher in Kelowna, BC, and in the final stages of a Master's of English degree at the University of British Columbia Okanagan (expected completion Spring/Summer 2016). His thesis is "Saying *God* with a Straight Face: Towards a Theological Understanding of Christian Soteriology in David Foster Wallace›s *Infinite Jest*." He has BA (History/English double major) and BEd degrees from UBCO. He is the co-host of The Great Concavity (a podcast dedicated to discussing the work of David Foster Wallace), and was a weekly contributing guide for the Infinite Winter community read between February and May of 2016.

Ben Leubner lives and teaches in Bozeman, Montana. He writes mainly on modernist literature and twentieth century poetry and poetics.

Tony McMahon is a PhD candidate at RMIT University in Melbourne, Australia. In September 2014, he presented a paper for the Infinite Wallace conference at the Sorbonne in Paris. In May 2015, he presented at Illinois State University's DFW15 conference, before traveling to the David Foster Wallace archives at the Harry Ransom Centre at the University of Texas, where he conducted research on Wallace and punk. The published proceedings of the Paris conference will feature a chapter by him titled "David Foster Wallace and Music: the Grunge Writer and the Hitherto Criminally Overlooked Importance of Signifying Rappers."

Brian Monday received his master's degree from Illinois State University, where he was awarded a Sutherland Fellowship, served as Production Director for the Unit of Contemporary Literature, and studied under Curtis White and David Foster Wallace. He has since taught English at Westosha Central High School, in Salem, Wisconsin, and has written a book of poems, *A Little Breath*, and a collection of short stories, *The Klein-Bottle Boy and His Ontological Dilemma*. Monday is currently studying the workshop critiques that Wallace offered him and hopes to collect other such critiques in a book that explores the nature of Wallace's teaching. He lives in Trevor, Wisconsin, with his wife and two sons.

Being a tenacious storyteller all his life, **Alex Bertacchi Passett** majored in English Studies at Illinois State University while also achieving a double minor in Spanish and Cinema Studies. Within the next two years, Passett's aspirations will gear towards attending graduate school at Illinois State, where he will be applying for a graduate assistantship with the Department of English. Writing every single day, Alex's fiction tends to gravitate towards character-driven plots, and he hopes to pave a way to becoming a novelist.

Ruben E. Rodriguez was born and raised in Peoria, Illinois and graduated from Illinois State University in 2013. He currently lives in Bloomington, where he reads, writes, works, and deals with the day to day struggle of living with a dog with a Napoleon complex.

Nathan Seppelt is an independent scholar and writer from Adelaide, Australia. His short fiction and nonfiction can be read on his blog at nathanseppelt.com.

Rob Short is a PhD candidate in English at the University of Florida. He is currently working on his dissertation, "David Foster Wallace and the Postmodern Novel of Ideas." His other areas of research include Twentieth-century American, British, and Irish Literature; Novel Studies; and finding useful ways to repurpose the computer skills he wasted years honing as a programmer in the service of this amorphous-but-allegedlyhighly-marketable thing his director calls "Digital Humanities."

Emily Spalding is honored to be included in the *Normal 2015* anthology! An avid playwright, screenwriter, and multi-instrumentalist, she finds herself calling upon her musical, literary, and artistic backgrounds for sources of inspiration. While she hails from Richmond, Virginia, New York City is her playground. Emily is a proud member of the Princeton University Class of 2020.

Tom Winchester holds an MFA in art criticism and writing from School of Visual Arts and has been published in the *Miami Rail*, *OMNI Reboot*, *Hyperallergic*, and *M/E/A/N/I/N/G*. He currently lives and works in Sarasota, Florida.

www.ingramcontent.com/pod-product-compliance
Lightning Source LLC
Chambersburg PA
CBHW071447150426
43191CB00008B/1263